Mini Habits
Smaller Habits, Bigger Results

by Stephen Guise

www.stephenguise.com

Primary blog – focusing, habits, small steps, etc.

www.minihabits.com

Supplemental book information

D1013919

Copyright and Disclaimers

Mini Habits™ by Stephen Guise

Preface (From Back Cover)

I had experimented with personal development strategies for a decade. When I accidentally started my first mini habit—and the changes I made were actually lasting—I realized the prior strategies I relied upon were complete failures. When something works, that which doesn't work is exposed. The science in *Mini Habits* exposes the predictably inconsistent results of most popular personal growth strategies, and reveals why mini habits are consistent.

A mini habit is a very small positive behavior that you force yourself to do every day; a mini habit's "too small to fail" nature makes it weightless, deceptively powerful, and a superior habit-building strategy.

Mini Habits will better equip you to change your life than 99% of the people you see walking around on this globe. People so often think that they are the reason they can't achieve lasting change; but the problem isn't with them—it's with their strategy. You can achieve great things without the guilt, intimidation, and repeated failure associated with such strategies such as "getting motivated," resolutions, or even "just doing it." To make changes last, you need to stop fighting against your brain. When you start playing by your brain's rules—as mini habits show you how to do—lasting change isn't so hard.

How This Book Is Structured

There are seven major parts in *Mini Habits*. The end goal of this book is to help you *permanently add healthy, habitual behaviors to your life.* The first three parts discuss habit-building, the brain, willpower, motivation, and how they relate to one another. The next two parts discuss logical and scientific conclusions about how to best utilize this information. The last three parts show you how to apply it. Here are the seven parts in greater detail:

1. Introduction To Mini Habits

Here, you'll find out what a mini habit is. This part includes the story of how I first made one push-up a full workout (which became a mini-phenomenon called "The One Push-up Challenge"). We'll also explore why habits are so critical to actively develop.

What it establishes: what a mini habit is, the importance of habits, and how I stumbled upon my first mini habit.

2. How Your Brain Works

In part two, we're going to take a look at the human brain. Understanding the brain can help tremendously in new habit formation, because you can employ superior strategies with this knowledge. We'll learn about the active and passive (i.e. conscious and subconscious) parts of the brain, and how they work together to shape our daily behavior.

What it establishes: the inner workings of the human brain as it relates to behavior change and creating new habits.

3. Willpower Vs. Motivation

We have two strategies for taking action—either get motivated so that we *want* to complete the task or force the issue by using willpower. Is one better than the other? Do we use both? Science reveals the winner and suggests the single best way to apply it.

What it establishes: why it's best to use willpower exclusively (with mini habits) and ignore motivation altogether.

4. The Strategy of Mini Habits

The first three parts laid the foundation for this concept of tiny, daily actions; in the next two parts, we'll discuss *why* that is the case and *how* it should work. Mini habits are most effective with the proper mindset, and this part gets you into that mindset.

What it establishes: the connection between the *Mini Habits* strategy and everything we've learned about habit change to this point.

5. The Mini Habits Difference

This part delves into the advantages of the *Mini Habits* strategy's differences and how it can work for you when others haven't.

What it establishes: all that makes mini habits uniquely effective.

6. Mini Habits – Eight Steps To Big Change

These eight steps will show you how to choose your habits, plan your journey, and take your first small steps forward. Each step is broken down into detail, explaining exactly why it's necessary, different strategies to employ, and how to best execute.

What it establishes: how to apply mini habits to your life, from the "I want to create a new habit" stage to success.

7. Eight Mini Habit Rules

This last part covers the eight rules of the *Mini Habits* strategy. These rules will keep you on track and ensure you maximize your potential and results.

What it establishes: the rules of mini habits that will help you get great results while avoiding habit-breaking mistakes.

***

Are you ready to discover how smaller habits lead to bigger results? I sure hope so, because I'm excited to show you. Let's go!

Contents

3. Reward Yourself Often, Especially After A Mini Habit

4. Stay Level-headed

5. If You Feel Strong Resistance, Back Off & Go Smaller

6. Remind Yourself How Easy This Is

7. Never Think A Step Is Too Small

8. Put Extra Energy and Ambition Toward Bonus Reps, Not A Bigger Requirement

Final Words — 116

An Optional Modification
Apply This Strategy Elsewhere
Want More?

Part 1

Introduction To Mini Habits

*"The journey of a thousand miles begins
with one step."*

Lao Tzu

Let's begin your first mini habit.

Read at least two pages of this book every day until you finish it. You may read more than that, but never less. It won't require much time or effort to read two pages, so there are no excuses. Now you can experience what it's like to *have* a mini habit as you read *about* mini habits.

Touch your nose right now. I'm serious. I'll explain later. Ok, now think about what the following truths mean for your life:

1. Big intentions are worthless if they don't bring results. For example, I can *say* that I will exercise for two hours every day, but if I never do it, the size of the intention doesn't matter. In fact, intention without action harms self-confidence.

2. People have been shown in studies to chronically overestimate their self-control ability.[1]

These two simple points reveal why so many people struggle to change. They have big ambitions, but overestimate their ability to make themselves do what it takes to change. It's a mismatch between desire and ability.

Here are two more facts to consider:

1. Doing a little bit is *infinitely* bigger and better than doing nothing (mathematically and practically speaking).

2. Doing a little bit *every day* has a greater impact than doing a lot on one day. How much greater? Profoundly so, because a little bit every day is enough to grow into a lifelong foundational habit, and those are a big deal, as you'll see.

If these statements seem reasonable to you, the main conclusion to draw is that small intentions are better than big intentions. Interesting, right? We're just getting started.

Have you ever felt stuck? Have you ever tried to change yourself for the better and failed? Have you done it over and over again, and even stopped trying for long periods of time?

We've all been there, I think, but let me ask you these more interesting questions.

What if your failure to take action and stick to your plan was never a problem with you, but a problem with your strategy—the strategy that most of the world uses and endorses? And what if the science about human behavior, willpower, and the brain suggested a better alternative for sticking to your plans—one that is rarely practiced or promoted? And what if a shift to this new strategy changed everything for you, and no matter how you felt, you knew you could take action, reach your goals, form good habits, and change your life?

Welcome to the world of mini habits.

It all sounds overblown, I know, but you just read my mini-autobiography up there. This is the exact reality and the revelation that transpired for me starting in late 2012. The previous ten years of my life were a constant search and struggle to grow, with disappointing results. But then I tried something that produced a breakthrough unlike I had ever experienced before, so I scrambled to understand exactly *why* this odd strategy worked so well, and I was (and am still) amazed at how everything fits together. And now here's this book.

We're quick to blame ourselves for lack of progress, but slow to blame our strategies. Then we repeat them over and over again, trying to make them work. But here's the thing—if you fail using a particular strategy more than a few times, you need to try another one. It doesn't matter if it works for everyone else if it doesn't work for you! This is a lesson I wish I had learned years ago.

I asked you to touch your nose earlier because I wanted you to prove something to yourself. First, notice that there's no reward for touching your nose. Second, consider that you did it anyway because you can. If you didn't do it then, do it now so the following words apply to you (or choose another small action if you're one of those stubborn types).

You were able to touch your nose because the resistance you felt was not stronger than your willpower. Congratulations! You are now *Mini Habits* approved.

That was a rudimentary exercise in willpower. If you can force yourself to touch your nose, then you can have success with this book's strategy. I'm not joking. This book exists because I did one push-up on December 28, 2012. My ability to do 16 pull-ups in a row and my improved physique result from that same push-up. I read and write every single day because of that push-up. That one push-up was the first step that lead to all of these great changes in my life.

Every great accomplishment rests on the foundation of what came before it; when you trace it back, you'll see one small step that started it all. Without that one push-up, I'd still be struggling to get motivated to go to the gym, and to read and write consistently. That push-up led me to discover this new strategy, which turned into these great benefits. Are you ready to hear the story of the one small action that changed everything for me?

How It Began: The One Push-up Challenge

I'm thinking about naming it "the golden push-up."

It was December 28, 2012 and the new year was near. Like many others, I reflected on 2012 and was not impressed. I wanted to live better in 2013; my top desire was fitness. I wasn't about to set a New Year's resolution though—I had decided against them years ago, because they have an abysmal 8% success rate.[2]

I felt like I had better odds of winning in Las Vegas than in life. Ever since my later years of high school, I had tried to make exercise a habit. But for ten years it never stuck, despite my efforts. Those aren't the types of results that instill confidence in oneself! My motivational bursts to change would usually last me about two weeks before I'd quit for one reason or another. Sometimes there was no reason; I'd just stop. Wanting to do something before the arbitrary January 1st starting point associated with resolutions, I decided to start by exercising right there on the spot for 30 minutes.

But I stood motionless. I couldn't get motivated. I went through my usual "get motivated" routine. *Come on Stephen. True champions put in the extra work.* I tried listening to up-tempo music, visualizing myself with a great beach body, etc. Nothing worked. I felt out of shape, lethargic, and worthless to the point that I couldn't do anything. A 30-minute workout looked like Mount Everest. The idea of exercise was wholly unappealing. I felt so defeated, and I was.

It wasn't just the time or the effort of a 30-minute workout that intimidated me, it was the total amount of work I needed to put in to reach my fitness desires. It was the vast distance between here and there. A year's worth of workouts weighed on my mind. I felt guilty, overwhelmed, and discouraged before I had even done anything!

The Turning Point

Months earlier, I had read a fantastic creative thinking and problem-solving book called *Thinkertoys* by Michael Michalko. One of the creative thinking "toys" he talks about is called False Faces. In False Faces, you consider the opposite of what you're currently thinking, and see what creative ideas emerge from that. A crude example: instead of building a skyscraper, what if you built a structure deep into the earth? This generates creative ideas by forcing your mind to zoom out and see the spectrum of possibilities.

I had a problem to solve, and this technique popped into my head, so I thought about the opposite of a 30-minute workout. Eating ice cream and watching TV would be one opposite of exercise. Then I considered that a full 30 minutes just seemed like *such* a huge challenge in that moment (i.e. Everest). Another opposite, I considered, could be the size of the workout. What if instead of this big 30-minute commitment of sweat and discomfort, I did a single push-up? I would have no requirement to do more—just one push-up. It was the true opposite of my Mount Everest workout.

I laughed off the idea, literally. *How pathetic! One push-up isn't going to help anything. I really need to put in more work than that!* But every time I switched back to my first plan, I couldn't do it. After I got tired of failing to do the 30-minute workout, I thought, *Whatever, I'll do one push-up.* I got down on the ground, did one push-up, and changed my life for good.

When I got into push-up position, I noticed it was exactly the same as the start to an actual 30-minute workout. I did my push-up; my shoulder popped, my elbows needed WD-40; it felt like my muscles were waking up from a 24-year nap. But without pause I did a few more, because I was already in position. Every push-up was rough on my underused muscles and stubborn brain.

As I stood up, I concluded that it was better than nothing. Mind you, I still felt like quitting at this point. But then I had the idea to set another small challenge of one pull-up. It was too easy to turn down. I got my pull-up bar set up and did one. Then I did a few more. *Interesting*, I thought, *this is hard, but not as hard as I was making it out to be.*

My muscles were warming up. My motivation to do more had definitely increased, but it was so low to start with (and I was so out of shape) that I still had plenty of internal resistance. I continued on with the same strategy, going as small as necessary to continue. During one push-up session in my workout, I had to set seven micro goals like so: *ok, one more, ok, two more, now one more.* Every time I baited myself with a beyond-easy challenge, I met or exceeded it. It felt nice to meet a goal for a change.

When I finished, I had exercised for 20 minutes, and felt great about it. Usually at this point in a workout, I'd complete a 10-minute ab exercise video. When the thought crossed my mind, my brain promptly shot it down like a digital bird in the video game Duck Hunt, saying, "You had your fun, but don't push your luck." But you can probably guess what I did next.

I decided to set up my floor mat. Brain accepted that. Then I decided to find an ab video. Brain accepted. Then I decided to press play. 10 minutes later, my abs were ablaze. It's important to note that these were individual decisions. At no point did I have the full weight of completing a 10-minute ab-ripping program on my mind. If I had, I would have never done it.

The day after I had turned one push-up into the impossible-seeming 30-minute workout, I wrote "The One Push-up Challenge." It turned into one of my most popular posts to date. I still receive messages from people telling me how it's helped them to exercise consistently.

As 2013 went on, I continued to require one push-up per day from myself. Usually, I did more than one. But one day I forgot until I was already in bed. So I flipped over onto my stomach and did my one push-up in bed. I laughed at the thought of meeting the daily requirement at the last second. It sounds meaningless, but it actually felt amazing to succeed so easily and keep the streak alive. Later, I would see how important this was for my success.

I noticed two things. First, just a few push-ups a day *does* make a difference in how you feel, physically and mentally. I felt stronger and my muscles were better conditioned. Second, I realized that exercise was becoming habitual; even with such a wimpy challenge, I was doing *something* every day. Regular workouts were becoming easier. With this positive experience under my belt, I was curious whether a scientific explanation existed for why super small steps were working better for me than larger goals. Research showed that there is indeed, and you'll see it peppered throughout this book. There's no single study that says "Mini habits are the answer." Instead, this philosophy of habit-building rests on the shoulders of dozens of studies that have revealed the nature of willpower and the brain, and what it takes to take consistent action.

Starting in late June, I made the jump from home to gym, and I've built a few pounds of muscle since then. On September 20th, I realized the potential of this formula for other areas of my life, such as reading and writing. I've amazed myself since then by increasing my productivity and staying in great shape. All of the things I've been wanting are happening now. Recently, I've even started eating mega salads just because I want to do it. When you invest in yourself in key areas like fitness and learning, you tend to do it in other areas too.

For Good Habits Only

Before we get any further, I want you to understand that this book will not help you quit smoking or control a gambling addiction. Mini habits are for good habits only—adding positive behaviors to your life to enrich it for years. Breaking bad habits and making good habits do have the same goal—replacing a default behavior with a better behavior. With bad habits, your primary motivation for change is an *away* response *from* something bad. With good habits, your primary motivation for change is a *toward* response *to* something good. Mini habits focuses on the toward response.

Changing deeply-rooted *active* bad habits like substance addiction involves a different psychological process and may require professional assistance. That said, if you're looking for a long-term play to help with *passive* bad habits such laziness, fear, or wasting time, then this book can help you tremendously. Passive bad habits can often be marginalized by incorporating good habits into your life. How can you continue with your bad habits if you spend all of your time on good ones? And honestly, adding good habits this way is pretty easy to do. Quick fixes are often bogus, but when you've literally been fighting against your brain for a decade (or more for some of you), then a strategy that works *with* your brain will be easy in comparison. With the right knowledge and strategy to change, what previously seemed impossible becomes rather straightforward and possible. It's like trying to open a locked door —it's only easy if you have the right key (or are a locksmith or thief, but now the analogy is too complicated).

That said, those covered in darkness (probably because of their bad habits) need light in their life too. If your life is a complete mess of bad habits, adding in some good habits can change you. Darkness is not something that exists on its own—it's the name we give for the *absence* of light. Perhaps people have bad habits because they lack the light of good habits, which permits a dark void in their life. When you add good habits into your life, it illuminates another possible path, restores your confidence, and gives you hope. It also serves as a brilliant foundation from which to build.

This information doubles as a life philosophy that demonstrates, explains, and celebrates that the first step forward is always the most important one...by far. In other words, it can help you in other areas besides your habits. I don't merely hope that this book will help you, I'm confident that it will...as confident as I am that most people's New Year's resolutions will fail. That is, it's a high statistical probability. With mini habits, you can join the ranks of people who change their lives in the most unbelievable way.

A Brief Synopsis Of Mini Habits

Since I refer to mini habits throughout the book, I want to briefly explain the concept. A mini habit is basically a *much* smaller version of a new habit you want to form. 100 push-ups daily is minified into one push-up daily. Writing 3,000 words daily becomes writing 50 words daily. Thinking positively all the time becomes thinking two positive thoughts per day. Living an entrepreneurial lifestyle becomes thinking of two ideas per day (among other entrepreneurial things).

The foundation of the *Mini Habits* system is in "stupid small" steps. The concept of small steps is nothing new, but how and why they work have not been adequately dissected. Of course, small steps are relative too; a small step for you could be a giant leap for me. Saying "stupid small" clarifies it, because if a step sounds stupid relative to the most you can do, it's perfect.

The power of the *Mini Habits* system is in the application, mindset, built-in positive feedback looping, naturally increasing self-efficacy, and of course, leveraging small steps into habits. This will be explained, but it's also built in; it's a simple system with a complex, smart backing.

The way we act on these mini habits is by using a small amount of willpower to force ourselves to do something. It doesn't take a lot of willpower to do one push-up or come up with a couple of ideas.

The benefit from following the *Mini Habits* system is surprisingly big results. First, there's a great chance that you'll do "bonus reps" after you meet your small requirement. This is because we already desire these positive behaviors, and starting them reduces internal resistance. The second benefit is the routine. Even if you don't exceed your small requirement, the behavior will begin to become a (mini) habit. From there, do bonus reps or scale the habit up. Another benefit is constant success. A bank may be too big to fail, but mini habits are *too small to fail*; and so they lack the common destructive feelings of guilt and inadequacy that come with goal failure. This is one of the very few systems that practically guarantees success every day thanks to a potent encouragement spiral and always-attainable targets. Mini habits have made me feel unstoppable; prior to starting mini habits, I felt unstartable.

To summarize, a mini habit is a VERY small positive behavior that you force yourself to do every day. Small steps work every time, and habits are built by consistency, so the two were meant to be together. Hey, it's still a better love story than *Twilight*.

About Habits And The Brain

Why not just use small steps in daily life? Well, you absolutely should! But habits are the framework of your life, so to ignore them is a pretty big mistake. When I discovered the power of small steps from the One Push-up Challenge, I felt like a superhero who had just discovered his superpower and wondered, *How can I use this for the greatest good?* Habits were the answer.

This book focuses on using small steps for habits because there is nothing more important than your habits. A Duke University study concluded that about 45% of our behavior is from habit.[3] They are even more important than this 45% stake suggests, because habits are frequently repeated behaviors (often daily), and this repetition adds up to big benefits or big damage in the long run.

The habit of writing 1,000 words per day would result in 365,000 words written a year. That's equal to seven 50,000-word novels. Though it would be shy of Leo Tolstoy's 580,000-word behemoth *War and Peace* (that guy sure had a lot to say).

Consider these classic novels that weigh in at about 50,000 words each:

- Douglas Adams' *The Hitchhiker's Guide To The Galaxy* (46,333 words)

- Stephen Crane's *The Red Badge Of Courage* (50,776 words)

- F. Scott Fitzgerald's *The Great Gatsby* (50,061 words)

Now, you may not write a novel of such world renown on the first try (or the first 100), but if you write seven per year, you'll have quite a few attempts to perfect your craft, right?

More potentially life-changing habits:

- The habit of exercising 20 minutes a day is enough to change your physique.

- The habit of eating healthier foods may add years to your life (and give you more vitality throughout).

- The habit of rising one hour earlier each morning to read would give you 365 extra hours more per year. At the average reading speed of 300 words per minute, this extra time would allow you to read 6,570,000 words, or 131 more 50,000-word books per year. That's a LOT of books, and a sure way to increase your knowledge.

There are also less concrete examples such as thinking positively and being grateful that can have a dramatic impact on your life. With mini habits, this "store" of life perks is now open for business. Choose your favorite habits and add them to your cart. For more mini habit ideas, visit minihabits.com. But wait, come back here! You've got to finish the book before you get too carried away. There's important information ahead that will help you succeed.

***

Merriam-Webster's dictionary defines a habit as "a usual way of behaving: something that a person does often in a regular and repeated way." Since I tend to think in terms of resistance and willpower, I say it's "a behavior that's easier to do than not to do."

Habits are not directly accessible—you can't immediately create or remove one right now. They are molded over time by repetition.

What Do Habits Look Like In The Brain?
Neural pathways are communication channels in the brain, and these pathways are what habits "look like" in the physical world.

Here's how it works: once a habit's assigned neural pathway is triggered by a thought or external cue, an electrical charge fires along the pathway in your brain, and you'll have an urge or thought to engage in the habitual behavior. For example, if you take a shower immediately after waking up every day, you'll have a neural pathway associated with that behavior. You'll wake up, the "shower neurons" will fire, and you'll walk to the shower like a zombie—no thinking required! This is the magic and the curse of having habits, depending on if they are good or bad. As a habit becomes more ingrained, the associated neural pathway will literally get thicker and stronger. Yikes!

Knowing this information simplifies and clarifies our goal. We want to create and strengthen specific neural pathways with repetition. It sounds easy when put this way, but we'll have to overcome innate human limitations to do it. Many standard habit strategies you'll find don't take these proven limitations into account, underestimate how severe they are, or make vague and unhelpful statements like, "It's going to be hard; you've got to want it." Without a solid plan to handle these limitations, you'll suffer from burnout or inconsistency and give up early, even if you go in "fired up." Can you tell I'm a bit anti-motivational? That's because it failed me for ten years, but we'll get to that later.

Habits Are A Matter Of Life And... Stress?
While we're discussing the importance of habits, consider stress.

Today's world runs at a faster pace than ever before, and we all seem to be more stressed out as a result. Life is imperfect, and it's impossible to navigate it without some stress. The question that most people never think to ask is, "How does stress impact my habits?"

Stress has been shown to increase habitual behavior—for better or worse! Two experiments at UCLA and one at Duke University found that stress increased people's gravitation toward habitual behavior. Based on her study in the *Journal of Personality and Social Psychology,* [4] Professor Wendy Wood argues: "People can't make decisions easily when stressed, are low in willpower or feeling overwhelmed. When you are too tired to make a decision, you tend to just repeat what you usually do."[5] This holds true for both good and bad habits and is a crucial insight for their importance in our lives.

Just imagine for a second now what can happen if your bad habits stress you out. It's the perfect recipe for a negative feedback loop. Your stress triggers a bad habit, which triggers guilt, internal angst, and more stress, which triggers the habit again. But now imagine what could happen if your habits are naturally stress-relieving, such as exercise. In this case, your stress will chauffeur you to the gym, and the exercise will help you to relieve tension. The difference in impact on your life is mind-blowing, as one puts you in a positive position to succeed despite life's harsh occurrences, while the other constantly threatens to drop you into a negative spiral. Being a football fan, I think of the big swings in games where one team is about to score a touchdown from the one-yard line, but the quarterback throws an interception that the other team returns for a touchdown. That's not just seven points for the other team, it takes away the probable seven points his team was going to gain! It's a 14-point swing. Because of stress, all habits tend to be "14-point swings."

The other implication this has for us is in the difficulty of change. Higher amounts of stress make it more challenging for us to change our lives. As Professor Wood says, "You tend to just repeat what you usually do." If stress makes us run to our habits, then it also makes us run *away* from everything else, including that new positive behavior that we'd like to make into a habit. You can't see it, but I'm smiling right now. The standard habit formula crumbles when we're stressed because our existing habits get stronger, but the *Mini Habits* system won't fail you here.

How Long Does It Take To Form A New Habit?
It depends. Anyone who tells you differently is repeating what they've heard (which is wrong).

It is NOT 21 or 30 days. For Pete's and everyone else's sake, I want to put this up on every billboard! The 21-day habit myth was possibly started by Dr. Maxwell Maltz, a plastic surgeon. Dr. Maltz reportedly found that amputees took about 21 days to get used to the loss of a limb. So he argued that 21 days was how long it took for people to adjust to any life changes. Really, Doc? I would argue that coping with losing a limb and trying to drink more water are not the same type of experience. And I'll add that they're both quite different from trying to do 150 push-ups a day.

The most-cited viable study on habit formation duration was published in 2009 in the *European Journal Of Social Psychology*.[6] Each participant chose an "eating, drinking or activity behavior to carry out daily in the same context (for example 'after breakfast') for 12 weeks." And what did they find?

The average time for a behavior to become habit was 66 days. But the range was wild, from 18 to 254 days, showing that there is huge variation in people's time to reach habit automaticity, and that it can end up taking a very long time in some cases. 21- and 30-day challenges are popular, but they're highly unlikely to form many types of habits. Drinking a glass of water every day could fall into the 21-day window, but something more challenging like 100 sit-ups daily could take a couple hundred days or more to become habit.

That's the bad news. The good news is that habits aren't snap on, snap off—if you do 100 sit-ups for 60 days, day 61 will be much easier for you than day one was, even if it isn't completely automatic yet. Building a habit is like riding a bike up a steep incline that levels out, peaks, and goes down. To start, you have to push with all the force your legs can muster. It gets progressively easier after that, but you must keep pedaling until you reach the top of the hill or you'll go backwards and lose your progress.

In my experience, the first sign of habit formation is decreased resistance, which makes perfect sense. Our mind communicates internally by sending electrical impulses through these neural pathways, and we know that electricity always takes the path of least resistance. Like this concept, our brain prefers to perform habits because they have existing pathways and known rewards. But new behaviors are unproven, risky, and have no neural pathway. So when you don't have a solid pathway for this behavior yet, you have to manually override the typical behavior. As you do it more, the "baby neural pathway" will start to grow, and over time, it will compete with the previous behavior.

As for the process, it doesn't matter how long a habit takes you to form because the goal is to do it forever anyway. Why would you want to exercise for 6 months and quit when you reached your goal? Wouldn't it be disheartening to regress after that point? What really matters is recognizing the signs of a behavior becoming a habit, after which you can switch your focus to something else and still maintain the behavior.

One more interesting note from the 2009 study: researchers concluded that missing a day did not derail a habit, physiologically speaking; one day didn't make or break the process. But psychologically, missing a day *can* be a problem if you let it. It's better not to miss a day, but keep this fact in mind if you do—it might stop you from getting discouraged and losing your progress.

Part 2

How Your Brain Works

"I am a brain, Watson. The rest of me is a mere appendix."

Arthur Conan Doyle (Sherlock Holmes)

In this chapter, I've taken the liberty of slicing the brain up into two different entities—the subconscious brain and the conscious brain. The brain is *far* more complex than that with many parts, but for our purposes, this is sufficient.

Let this next point seep into the deepest depths of your mind and lodge there permanently. Never forget this:

Repetition is the language of the (subconscious) brain.

(Hint: If you *repeat* it, you won't forget it. And there's the first and last brain joke.)

The goal in creating habits is to change your brain with repetition. But the brain will resist changes unless they reward it handsomely. So really, the two keys to habit change as far as the brain is concerned are repetition and reward. It will be more willing to repeat something when there is a reward.

Have you ever driven a car without power steering? You have to turn the wheel several rotations just to get a small response from the car. Our brains respond to change like cars without power steering. Each iteration results in a negligible difference, but repeated consistently, these small alterations can create a big change in your brain (and your life).

Your subconscious brain loves efficiency; this is *why* we have habits. When you repeat a behavior over time, your brain learns to automate the process. It's more energy efficient to automatically do something than to manually weigh your options and decide to act the same way every time. When you make a decision very quickly, it is probably from habit, even if you think you're actively deciding. In a way, you made the decision a while ago. Choosing your favorite ice cream flavor is one example.

Slow-Changing, Stable Brains

The human brain is slow-changing and stable; it has routines and a framework that allow it to respond consistently to the world. Having a slow-changing brain is frustrating at times, but overall, it's highly beneficial. Imagine if your personality and life could transform overnight—you would go crazy!

Once you successfully develop new healthy habits, everything becomes easier. You can get up, eat your healthy breakfast, and go to the gym every morning automatically instead of conducting a drawn-out battle with your brain. You can do the right things with little effort. For many, this feels like a daydream. They only know the dark side of stability: how the brain compels them to eat junk food, watch TV, smoke, and bite their nails. But good habits are as amazing as bad habits are dreadful.

I know exercise is a habit for me because my identity has changed with it. It would feel odd and unsatisfying in a *that's not me* kind of way if I didn't go to the gym a few times per week. Last year, however, my identity was as a person who did *just enough* to stay in average shape. Both scenarios emerge from habit. Since 45% of our behavior is automatic regardless of what we do, we might as well make it beneficial to our lives and goals. In order to do that expertly, we need to understand the two primary players in the brain.

A Stupid Repeater & A Smart Manager

Most of your brain is stupid. Well, not yours specifically—a certain part of every human brain is stupid, in the sense that it doesn't consider lung cancer while you smoke or the perks of great abs before you exercise. Worse, this is the *strong* part of your brain that usually gets its way long term. It recognizes and repeats patterns until told otherwise. It's called the basal ganglia.

There is another section of your brain, however, that is really smart. It's called the prefrontal cortex and it's located behind your forehead. It's the "manager" that understands long-term benefits and consequences, and thankfully, it has the ability to override the basal ganglia. It handles short-term thinking and decision-making too.

Just now, we've covered the two critical tools involved in habit change—the basal ganglia and the prefrontal cortex. I like the way Psychologist Dr. David Nowell differentiates the prefrontal cortex from the rest of the brain. He says that everything except the prefrontal cortex determines "what is" and the prefrontal cortex focuses on "what could be."

The only way to create habits is to teach the rest of your brain to like what the prefrontal cortex wants. The prefrontal cortex is what resists chocolate cake (if at all possible), wants to learn French, wants to be fit, and would like to write a book someday. It's the conscious part of your brain that you'd identify as "you." But the problem is that tires out easily. Perhaps more accurately, because its functions are so powerful, it's an energy hog that tires *you* out. And when you tire out (or are stressed, as we covered), the repetitious part takes over.

The basal ganglia isn't conscious or aware of higher-level goals that are unique to humans. But it *is* an efficient pattern-repeater that saves us energy. So while it may not be "intelligent" like the prefrontal cortex, it is an incredibly important part of the brain. And once we train the basal ganglia to do positive behaviors automatically, we're really going to love it.

This is the system we all have to work with. It sounds poorly designed at first, as the smart prefrontal cortex has less stamina than the thoughtless, repeating basal ganglia does, but it's actually brilliant when you know how to work it. How do clever weaklings ever overcome their dumb, strong counterparts? I'll give you a hint —it's not through brute physical force. I'm sure you already know that, perhaps because you are now recalling the failed attempts of your conscious mind to control your subconscious mind by brute force or willpower. The answer, of course, is to employ *smart strategies* to overcome the prefrontal cortex's natural weaknesses.

The Prefrontal Cortex—Your Defense Against Automated Behavior

In order to understand the prefrontal cortex better, we're going to look at what happens when it's gone. How does a brain operate without one? Not well. The upcoming study shows what the prefrontal cortex does, as well as what the rest of the brain does. When you remove something, you can see the impact of what it did and also how the parts operate without its influence.

Francois Lhermitte was a French neurologist who examined patients with damaged frontal lobes. What he found in the following study was evidence that the brain's operation changes drastically without its "manager," the prefrontal cortex (which is part of the frontal lobes). [7]

There are two groups of interest in Lhermitte's study—people with damaged frontal lobes and people with healthy frontal lobes. In the experiment, the subjects would sit across from an examiner and ask interview-style questions. The examiner's task was to display indifference to the interviewer, refuse to respond to their questions, and occasionally perform random and puzzling gestures. He'd thumb his nose, give a military salute, fold paper and put it into an envelope, chew paper, sing, tap his leg, whimper, and more. (Ha! Science is fun[ny]!) Here's what they found.

Healthy-lobed people, as one would expect, found his behavior odd. In purely scientific terms, the response was "what's wrong with this dude?" Many of the younger participants laughed. And when asked if they thought to imitate him, they said, "No, not at all." [8]

But here's where it gets very interesting. Almost all people with frontal lobe damage *did* imitate the examiner's absurd gestures—they imitated him with great precision and without fail. For example, the men willingly urinated on a wall in front of others without any hint of surprise or concern. When they lacked the ability to imitate him exactly (such as not having paper to fold or chew), they were said to find ways to compensate "perfectly." [9]

From the study: "When interviewed after an examination, all [damaged lobe] patients could remember the examiner's gestures and, when questioned as to the reason for their imitative behavior, replied that because the examiner had made the gesture, they felt they had to imitate him. On being told that they had not been told to imitate the gestures, their answer was that obviously since the gestures had been made, they must be imitated. After being told not to imitate, most patients displayed the same IB (imitation behavior)." [10]

Those with damaged frontal lobes couldn't help but imitate the interviewer (even when asked not to). With damaged frontal lobes, it appears people lose the ability to make "override" decisions over their subconscious mind. The subconscious is almost like a different entity, a machine. Also interesting is that the normal participants forgot some of the gestures of the examiner, but those with damaged frontal lobes remembered *every single one*. This suggests that the presence of healthy frontal lobes (which again, contain the essential prefrontal cortex) steals some of our focus away from subconscious pattern recognition and can inhibit or initiate behavior. This is why we call it the "manager." It oversees automated operations and steps in when it sees something that could be done better. Now for the flip side—what happens when it's the basal ganglia that isn't functioning properly?

The Basal Ganglia—Your Pattern Detector

Your brain's basal ganglia is technically a group of nuclei that act as a single unit, and plays a central role in habit formation and procedural learning.

But research also indicates that the brain's many systems interact with each other in complex ways and the basal ganglia can't necessarily be isolated as being "the habit part of the brain."[11] Neuroscience, while helpful, cannot completely explain *exactly* how the brain works. That's not to say it's deceitful or inaccurate, but rather a small glimpse into a big mystery. The brain's workings are so intricate and complex that modern science still has a lot to learn. That said, knowing the basal ganglia is the main player in habit formation is useful. When combined with experience, experimentation, and good sense, our limited knowledge of the brain's workings is a powerful ally for personal growth.

Lhermitte's study on people with dysfunctional or damaged frontal lobes showed us the importance of the executive function of the brain, which can prevent us from robotically doing undesirable things. But what happens when it's the basal ganglia that's damaged or functioning improperly? There's a study on that too. It suggests that a damaged or malfunctioning basal ganglia causes you to lose your ability to have any habits.[12]

Researchers gathered people of three classifications—healthy people, Parkinson's disease patients, and those with memory problems. Parkinson's disease patients are those whose brains struggle to deliver the neurotransmitter dopamine to the basal ganglia due to cell death. This causes dysfunction of the basal ganglia.

Participants were given four cards with random shapes on them, and asked to predict whether each card meant rain or sunshine. It would be very difficult to consciously form relationships between the cards and results, but there was a subtle pattern that could be picked up subconsciously. There were 50 trials, and after about ten trials, both normal participants and memory loss participants gradually improved their guessing percentage from 50% to 65-70%; their subconscious mind picked up the patterns that suggested rain or sunshine. The Parkinson's disease participants, however, did not improve from 50%.   Without a healthy basal ganglia, their brain couldn't detect patterns (and thus, it would be hard for them to develop new habits).

From these studies, we can see the brain is, in vastly oversimplified terms, a two-part system of executive decision-making and pattern-recognition for automated behaviors. The management functions of the prefrontal cortex can be dynamic and responsive, but they use up a lot of energy (and willpower). The automation functions of the basal ganglia are effective and efficient. They save us energy and take care of tasks that don't need constant monitoring.

This leads into the next important consideration—how do we get ourselves to do things consistently with these two brain components?

Before a behavior becomes habit, the two ways to get yourself going are motivation and willpower. Before you read this next chapter, say your final goodbyes to motivation, because you're not going to need it anymore.

Part 3

Motivation Vs. Willpower

"Emotions will either serve or master,
depending on who is in charge."

Jim Rohn

I'm about to unleash fury on motivation as a starting strategy, but motivation and willpower aren't such "either or" strategies. They have an important relationship with each other that the chart below shows. The basic premise of this chapter is NOT that motivation is a bad thing, but that it's an *unreliable strategy* for lasting change.

Now, before you interrupt me to ask, "Hey, where are the mini habits?" give me a moment to explain. I've created a simple chart to show the relationship between willpower and motivation.

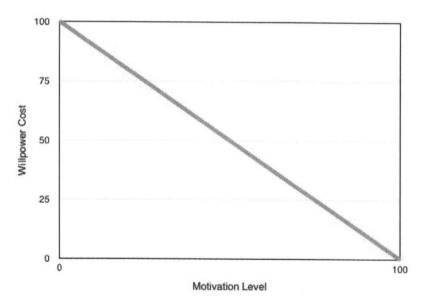

Chart explanation: Motivation is the x-axis, and willpower cost is the y-axis. When motivation is at its peak (lower right corner), willpower cost is zero or negligible. That's because you don't need to force yourself to do something you already *really* want to do. But when motivation drops to zero, strong internal resistance means that the willpower "cost" is high (upper left corner, where willpower cost is 100 and motivation is 0).

More about this relationship will be discussed in the willpower section, but all you need to know for now is that when you're not motivated to do something, the "willpower cost" skyrockets. And when willpower cost is high, it makes it difficult for you to sustain a behavior over time (and build it into a habit).

Now, let's take a hard look at "getting motivated," which dominates self-help literature despite being completely ineffective long term.

The Many Problems With "Getting Motivated"

Does getting motivated work? The answer is a maddening *sometimes*. At times, you can conjure up the motivation to exercise or write 2,000 words, but other times, you might end up taking a nap, watching TV, or drinking beer instead. This is a huge problem because...

If getting motivated is your strategy, you can't build habits.

We know that habits require consistent repetition. It wasn't until the 10th trial in the prior study that participants' brains picked up the pattern, and behaviors take much longer than that to be recognized.

Don't get me wrong here. Motivation is an important feeling with many benefits. But think of it as a bonus, something nice when it appears. I know some of you currently rely on getting motivated, so this next section's aim is to convince you to drop it. I genuinely want you to disown the concept for your own good, and here are the reasons why.

Motivation Is Unreliable
Motivation is unreliable because it's based on how you feel, and we've known for centuries that human feelings are fluid and unpredictable. Many things can alter your feelings: an event, blood sugar levels, depression, chemical fluctuations, hormones, health,

external stimuli, energy levels, beliefs, and cat vomit. In other words, *anything* can alter your feelings. Do you really want to place your hopes on something so... volatile? The #1 rule of any foundation is that it must be solid. Motivation is like building a house on liquid. (Don't you dare mention house boats—it ruins the analogy.)

Everyone has "off" days when energy is a bit lower. That means your motivation to do productive things will be lower too. This strategy makes us resort to things like motivational videos, articles, self pep-talks, and other short-term boosts.

And think about this: with a "get motivated" strategy, not only do you have to *be* motivated to do something, but you have to be *most* motivated to do it. So, to get motivated to exercise, you would have to want to exercise more than you want to eat chips and watch TV. You'll only succeed *sometimes*.

The activities that are good for us (eating raw broccoli, running 8 miles, and then eating more broccoli) are not the kinds of things that are easy to get motivated to do. The short-term rewards of raw broccoli and exercise have a *really hard time* competing with ice cream on the couch while watching a movie. My motivation to do the latter stays high.

You Won't Always Want To Get Motivated

The motivation theory of growth goes like this: if I want to do something, I don't need to force myself to do it (use willpower)! That's true. When you're motivated, it's easy to do things, and it doesn't require much, if any, willpower. Remember the chart at the beginning of this chapter? When you're fully motivated, willpower cost is zero. This seems like the best way at first, and even more so when you consider that willpower is a limited resource (covered later). This makes motivation highly desirable in theory, but as they say, "Every rose has its thorns, which cut your finger and make you curse in front of your nephew."

Problem: motivation is not easy (and sometimes nearly impossible) to cultivate on demand. Look no further than your own experiences to verify this. How easy has it been to motivate yourself when you're tired, sick, have a headache, feel "off," or just really want to do something else more fun? This idea of changing what you desire just by focusing on benefits really discredits the power and influence of how we feel. *It's hard to change your feelings by thinking.* It's when we have a lot of energy, a healthy mindset, and no major temptations that we succeed with motivation. But when the time comes to act and the scenario appears far less favorable, we'll decide to "do it tomorrow."

When I was tired and had a headache recently, there was no motivational phrase or thought that was going to make me work on this book. *I didn't want to get motivated either.* I wanted to sleep! Thankfully, I didn't rely on motivation.

There will be times in your life that you won't be motivated to get motivated. This means that you… bear with me here…don't want to want to want to exercise. (Yes, that was three "want tos" in a row!) That gives you a sense of how far away from taking action you can get with motivation-based thinking. Instead of just doing something, you have to want to do it, but sometimes you have build up motivation just to want to be motivated. It's every bit as crazy as it sounds. If you don't want to get motivated, and getting motivated was your strategy for doing things, you have lost the battle before it has begun. And your habits will die young.

Some People Habitually Think Motivation Is The Only Basis For Taking Action
As getting motivated has been established by parroting self-help writers as THE way to get yourself to take action and improve your life, few people question it. It's standard procedure. Motivational websites abound and thrive as people visit them for their "motivational fix." I'll admit that getting motivated is a better strategy than nothing, but nothing isn't hard to beat.

The desired effect of exercise, as an example, has three possible causes: motivation, willpower, or habit. Though every action is some combination of motivation and willpower, we tend to rely more on one or the other. Then there is that weird hybrid of trying to get motivated while saying you have to do it anyway (it usually comes to this when the battle is lost).

A destructive habit to have is believing that you have to be motivated to act. It's not a problem when you *would like to be motivated,* but when you *can't do anything unless you're motivated.* This is the perfect way to enter a laziness spiral. Being lazy makes you feel lazy, and if you always feel lazy and follow this motivation rule, then you'll continue to be lazy. There's no way out!

This idea that motivation precedes action can become deeply ingrained into a person's psyche. But there's no rule that says your feelings and actions must always match. It creates a confining, frustrating lifestyle.

Motivation Sets Us Up For Failure Through The Law Of Decreasing Enthusiasm
Ok, let's just say that you're able to get motivated to read for two hours every day. And say that you're able to do this for three weeks straight. At this point, you'd likely have a very weak habit beginning to form for this behavior. But since you've been relying on motivation, this crucial transition period will likely mean the end of your progress.

"The law of decreasing enthusiasm" isn't a real law, but a term I made up because it is more descriptive than the corresponding economic principle: "The Law of Diminishing Marginal Utility." This economic law says you will enjoy your 5th slice of pizza marginally less than your 4th slice, and your 4th slice less than your 3rd. When it comes to behavior repetition, the same sort of thing happens.

As a behavior begins its transition into habit, you will become less emotional about it. It will even begin to seem boring and mundane. Count on it. Jeremy Dean says in his book, *Making Habits, Breaking Habits*, that "A habit doesn't just fly under the radar cognitively; it also does so emotionally. [...] The act of performing a habit is curiously emotionless." [13] Dr. Wood and her colleagues noted this occurrence in a study they conducted at Texas A&M. When participants performed a habitual behavior, they were decidedly less emotional about it.[14] This is why thinking you need motivation to take action works against you in habit-building. Repetition doesn't make us more excited to do things, it makes us less excited; the perk habits offer is less resistance and more automaticity. Dean says, "The fact that habitual behavior doesn't stir up strong emotions is one of its advantages."[15] That's true, because anything dependent on human emotion is completely unreliable.

The initial excitement of starting something is an ally at first, but it becomes a formidable enemy when it fades and makes you wonder if something is wrong. You greatly reduce this risk, however, by not relying on your motivation and feelings in the first place.

It's great to be enthusiastic, but let's assume that mindset as a bonus, rather than the cue for taking action. It's better to do something because you choose to do it, a solid foundation that does not fluctuate wildly. Lack of enthusiasm after some time is counterintuitively a *positive sign* that control is moving to the more stable and automated basal ganglia.

This predictable enthusiasm decrease is one reason why you see so many people drop their exercise plans after January. Despite their success exercising, they'll notice, *I'm not feeling motivated anymore*, and stop going. Perhaps if they understood why they didn't feel motivated anymore, they'd be encouraged and continue.

As a main strategy, motivation might be good enough to get you by in life (maybe), but it's a poor choice compared to willpower.

While willpower is the best strategy, most people don't know how to use it and drain their willpower reserves quickly.

Despite everything I just said, don't worry; you can still enjoy your routines very much. You'll always be a human with feelings and emotions! I'm not asking you to never feel again. I'm asking you to never let your feelings stop you again.

Why Willpower Beats Motivation

Now that I've bashed motivation, I'm going to tell you how to get more of it. Contradiction? No, the reason I don't like motivation isn't because it's bad. For example, I need a baseline level of motivation to write these words. But motivation, through no fault of its own, has been masqueraded about town as the solution to personal growth. It's like if I told you carrots cured cancer. Carrots are good for you, but they won't likely cure anyone of cancer. So now this good thing (carrot) has been made into an enemy of the truth and is deceiving people. In this way, motivation is an evil carrot.

The *Mini Habits* willpower strategy is very conducive to motivation, which again, is good, but unreliable. I've found that by using willpower, motivation becomes more reliable; motivation comes fast when you take action first. There are three reasons why forcing yourself to take action with willpower is far better than trying to get motivated.

Willpower is Reliable
Unlike motivation-based techniques, willpower is extremely reliable. If you force yourself to do something no matter what, that's dependable. Of course, that's only if you can force yourself to do it. And it just so happens that these next two advantages of willpower make it even more reliable.

Willpower Can Be Strengthened

Unlike motivation, willpower can be strengthened like a muscle. Leading self-control researcher Professor Roy Baumeister found in 1999 that students who had exercised their willpower to improve their posture for two weeks, "showed a marked improvement on subsequent measures of self-control" compared to those who hadn't worked on their posture. [16] Another study found that a two-month aerobic exercise program resulted in improvements in other unrelated self-control activities. [17]

This is self-improvement gold. These studies suggest we can strengthen our very ability to improve ourselves!

But if something neither works the first time nor any time after, then you're spinning your wheels by continually trying. Motivation works sometimes, so it's tricky to evaluate. But if you look at your long-term results using motivation, you might see that it isn't working *consistently*. Motivation is not something that's easy to improve either because when your dog dies, your mood will darken; when you're tired or in a bad mood, you won't feel like exercising. You can, however, improve your ability to take action *despite* feeling resistance due to emotional trauma, lack of confidence, bad moods, or low energy levels. This is willpower.

Willpower Strategies Can Be Scheduled

If you rely on motivation, you will have a difficult time sticking to a schedule. When it's time to write, who knows if you'll be motivated or not? It's unpredictable and not calendar-friendly.

Using willpower, though, you can schedule an activity and do it whether you are motivated at the time or not. This allows for consistency, which is both habit- and calendar-friendly. Habits aren't made from a general plan to write when you can or exercise when the stars align. You've got to put the task on your calendar and do it, and that requires willpower.

The big question remains—how can we maintain consistent

success using willpower? To answer this question, let's summarize what science tells us about willpower and take it from there.

How Willpower Works

It used to be believed that willpower was an unlimited resource of, well...will. The idea was that if you wanted something enough, you would always have enough willpower to make yourself get it. That idea changed when Baumeister conducted a somewhat cruel study in 1996. [18] It started with 67 people in a room, which was promptly saturated with the tempting smell of freshly baked chocolate chip cookies. Then they brought the cookies and other chocolate treats into the room. Here is the cruel twist—only some of the participants were given chocolate treats to eat. Others, God help them, were given *radishes* to snack on instead! Even as a person who loves snacking on raw radishes, I feel their pain.

Scientists from the study humorously noted that quite a few of the radish eaters appeared to "exhibit clear interest in the chocolates, to the point of looking longingly at the chocolate display and in a few cases even picking up the cookies to sniff at them." (Ibid., 255) As I said, cruel.

After this, chocolate and radish participants alike were given a puzzle to solve. Those who ate radishes spent less than half the time attempting the puzzle as those who had consumed chocolate, and they attempted to solve it fewer times before giving up. It appears that having to eat radishes instead of cookies drained their will to continue struggling with the puzzle. Baumeister named this phenomenon "ego depletion." There have since been dozens of studies verifying the results from this groundbreaking study.

Decisions Drain Willpower Too!

Don't just blame the radishes. A self-control study found people who made a difficult decision earlier in the day were more likely to cave in to a temptation later, showing a decrease in self-control.[19] It seems that big decisions share the same pool of energy as our willpower. I imagine that anything that uses the prefrontal cortex could have this effect, because the prefrontal cortex handles short-term memory and current thinking. But you wouldn't typically think that making a tough decision could adversely affect your ability to resist ice cream or force yourself to exercise later in the day.

This means one thing—we've got to maximize our self-control reserves to be effective at changing ourselves. I include this just to show how other things can undercut our willpower reserves, making the philosophy behind mini habits even more important.

An Important Meta-Analysis Of Willpower
A meta-analysis is a "study of studies" that attempts to extract important conclusions from the body of related work on a given topic. This helps to smooth out possible aberrations from individual studies. If something holds true over dozens of properly conducted studies and thousands of participants, there's a very high probability of that data being reliable, illuminating, and useful.

In 2010, a meta-analysis of 83 studies was done on ego depletion. [20] Ego depletion essentially means the same thing as willpower or self-control depletion, so I will use these terms interchangeably. From this meta-analysis, the five biggest factors found to cause ego depletion were effort, perceived difficulty, negative affect, subjective fatigue, and blood glucose levels. These factors, then, are the five biggest obstacles that keep us from sustaining success with a willpower-based strategy. What do we do once we've exhausted our willpower? Is all hope lost then? According to the analysis, motivational incentives, training on self-control tasks, and glucose supplementation promoted better self-control of ego-depleted people. (Ibid.)

This gives us a wealth of information about how best to manage willpower. Here is an important motivation and willpower recap to set up this next part about the *Mini Habits* strategy for adding healthy habits to your life:

- New (or non-habit) behaviors are started by using motivation or willpower.

- Motivation isn't reliable, so it can't be the strategy for building habits.

- Willpower is reliable, but only if you don't run out of it.

- There are five main causes of willpower depletion: effort, perceived difficulty, negative affect, subjective fatigue, and blood glucose levels.

- If we can successfully overcome these five hurdles, we should find success.

In the next chapter, we'll discuss how mini habits fit everything we've covered so far, starting with these five main causes of willpower depletion.

Part 4

The Strategy Of Mini Habits

"It's not what we do once in a while that shapes our lives. It's what we do consistently."

Anthony Robbins

The *Mini Habits* strategy is forcing yourself to take 1-4 "stupid small" strategic actions every day. These actions are too small to fail, and too small to skip for special occasions. They serve dual purposes—to spark you to do more, and to become (mini) habits.

Now we'll look at how the *Mini Habits* strategy generally applies the principles we've learned thus far. The *specific* step-by-step instructions of the *Mini Habits* strategy comes two chapters after this one.

Using Willpower The Mini Habits Way

There was a study on ego depletion that found some correlation between believing willpower is limited and willpower becoming limited.[21] Those who didn't believe their willpower had a limit appeared to last longer in ego depletion activities. At first, this appears to be a strike against having mini habits, because they're designed around the assumption that willpower is limited (as shown in the meta-analysis). But let me explain why mini habits are a failsafe against either scenario.

If willpower is truly limited, then mini habits preserve it by starting small. But say that willpower is only limited by our belief that it's limited. What would that mean for mini habits? It's great news! You'll believe you have unlimited willpower with mini habits because they *require* almost no willpower. So in the case that you're bursting at the seams with willpower energy, mini habits will get you started and allow you to make great bonus progress. And in the case that you're completely exhausted and out of willpower, mini habits will get you started anyway and allow you to make the most of your capabilities at the time. The belief that you can take action no matter what is built into this theory, and it has not failed me a single time. Not once has my willpower been insufficient to complete a mini habit.

Now, I want to highlight again the five main causes of ego-depletion found from the 83 study meta-analysis mentioned earlier. The biggest five ego depletion drains were found to be (in no particular order):

- Effort

- Perceived difficulty

- Negative affect

- Subjective fatigue

- Blood glucose levels

Let's examine how all five of these willpower threats are mostly or completely nullified by mini habits.

Effort

Mini habits require very little actual effort. You're going to be doing one push-up, writing 50 words, reading two pages, or other very easy tasks. The subsequent bonus effort from overachieving is variable, meaning some days will be more productive than others. This is a natural structure that greatly reduces the chance for burnout. I've often planned to write 50 words and written 2,000 words. Other times, I've written closer to 50 just to meet the requirement.

The *Mini Habits* system is both rigid and flexible in strategic places. It's rigid in the beginning, forcing you to start, but it's flexible after that, allowing you to decide how much extra you want to do. The initial effort requires hardly any willpower.

Result with mini habits: very little ego depletion.

Perceived Difficulty

Mini habits have almost zero perceived difficulty by design, a primary benefit that compounds when you do extra. Remember when I talked about the big "mountain" that my 30-minute workout was to me? That workout had a *very high perceived difficulty*—my sense of the difficulty was greater than the actual difficulty. But when I decided to start with one push-up and continued in that fashion, the perceived difficulty dropped substantially. Setting mini goals is the best way to drop the perceived difficulty in any project.

Once you start and are free to continue, your perceived difficulty will be much lower due to the psychological impact of having already started. Just like in physics, the greatest inertia comes before the start of motion. Once you're in motion, everything gets easier as a result of momentum (and increased motivation).

Starting, even in a small way, also brings your mind into reality, and this is important. Before you take action, your mind can only imagine what a particular behavior would be like. My initial projection of a 30-minute workout was like scaling Mount Everest. It was wrong. When it comes to activities that require physical or mental effort, it's *extremely common* to overestimate how difficult they are. After I completed my 30-minute workout from force-starting with one push-up, I realized how absurd my initial perceived difficulty was.

Result with mini habits: very little ego depletion (even as you continue beyond your original target). The reason starting is the hardest part is because it carries the brunt of the weight of the commitment. Once we start, we feel as if we need to finish our original intention to count it as a success. This is why we tend not to start a project that intimidates us. We'd rather not start if we won't finish. This is why mini habits are so easy. The total intention is so small, there's no risk of quitting too early. By starting small and entering the reality of doing the work, your mind will see that one small step is not as difficult as it first seemed, and that taking the next step isn't difficult either.

Negative Affect

Negative affect simply means the experience of unpleasant feelings; it clearly played a role in the chocolate and radish study. Participants were tempted by the sight and smell of chocolate and were given the less desirable radishes. Being tempted with chocolate only to be denied even a taste was a very negative experience, perhaps more than we'd think (imagine someone presenting you with cookies and then withholding them. Ack!). As mini habits are for *adding* good things, negative affect is less relevant unless your action is directly replacing another pleasure. Eating radishes alone won't deplete willpower, for example, but when juxtaposed against chocolatey goodness, you bet they will!

Result with mini habits: typically no ego depletion. Even if you're replacing a pleasure with a mini habit, the commitment is so small that you won't feel negative affect from it. More often, you'll be replacing time-wasting behaviors with beneficial ones, which induces a positive feeling.

Subjective Fatigue

This is an interesting one, isn't it? It doesn't say fatigue; it says *subjective fatigue*, implying that we're not completely objective in our assessment of our own fatigue. It turns out that willpower is a battle of the mind, and according to some of these top willpower drainers, the battle appears to be between the perception of your strength relative to your task.

Mini habits thankfully come with a mini amount of subjective fatigue. Subjective fatigue depends on many factors, and a big one is how you see yourself stacking up against your goal. I've noticed that when my goal is large, my subjective fatigue worsens. This is logical, as the mind "looks ahead" to the upcoming work and perhaps feels the impact early. A recent study found that our imaginations are so powerful that they can change what we physically see and hear in the real world,[22] so it is not at all a stretch to think that expecting a heavy workload can impact our energy levels too. This idea was also supported by researchers in the meta-analysis, who noted, "expecting further acts of self-control exacerbated the effect [of ego depletion]."[23] I noticed that when my goal became just one push-up, my subjective fatigue shrunk. In fact, I felt I had *plenty* of energy to do a single push-up, and the thought that I could easily do *something*, albeit small, was energizing.

Result with mini habits: nothing can completely take away subjective fatigue, but mini habits mitigate it very well. In relation to your mini goals, you may feel a sense of empowerment and energy. Even when I've been exhausted (subjectively), I've still felt sufficiently energized to just read two pages or write 50 words. If you're wondering about the value in "only doing that much," it's high and it's covered later.

Blood Glucose Levels

Glucose (sugar) is your primary energy source. If you have low glucose in your blood, you're going to feel very tired. If it's dangerously low, you can even pass out. Your blood sugar levels are determined by genetics, diet, and lifestyle.

As for mini habits, they are independent of your blood sugar, but they can help to *preserve it* by being the most efficient way to spend your willpower energy. It is far more mentally energy efficient to break things down into small components that are easily "mentally digested" and less stressful. The goal of losing 100 pounds in a year is a constant energy drain and burden. And with this goal, it's possible to lose 50 pounds and feel like a failure. Why would anyone be interested in that?! One workout feels like a drop in the bucket, and it is in the grand scheme of your massive goal. It's hard to feel good after a workout when it represents almost nothing compared to your goal. With mini habits, though, willpower is preserved as much as possible, every step you take feels like success, and going beyond your goal feels even better than that. It's a system that makes you feel like a winner, because people who feel like winners act like winners.

Result with mini habits: while blood sugar levels are independent of mini habits, the fact that they are energy-efficient, willpower-efficient, and empowering psychologically, preserves blood sugar as much as any goal/habit strategy could. And if you're tired from low blood sugar, mini habits give you the best chance to take action anyway.

How Mini Habits Expand Your Comfort Zone

Right now you have a comfort zone. Imagine it as a circle. You're most comfortable inside of this circle, but outside of it are some of your desired goals. Outside the lines, you might see yourself physically fit and weighing less; you might envision books you've written or books you'd like to read; a happier version of you with fewer negative thoughts; a version of you who cooks more meals at home; or whatever else you're interested in improving. These are outside of your comfort circle because they require some discomfort to achieve (due to straying from your basal ganglia's current routines).

The common way people go about this change is diving in and trying a "whatever it takes to succeed" strategy. This is like sprinting well outside of your comfort circle and fighting to stay there. That's when your subconscious brain says, *this is interesting, but I'm really uncomfortable with this huge change*, and it forces you back inside your comfort circle when your motivation and willpower can no longer support you out there.

Mini habits are like walking to the outer edge of your circle and taking one step outside of the boundaries. You're in less comfortable territory here, but not by much, because you know taking one step back will put you back inside your comfort circle. And maybe for the first few times, you will step right back inside your comfort circle (only meeting your mini requirement). But when you continue to step outside the circle, your subconscious will get comfortable with it and your circle will expand (we're talking about a mini habit forming here). This expansion, unlike the sprints in the prior example, can *permanently* change your boundaries, and it is the magic bullet of mini habits. Because while I hope you get the urge to explore your outer boundaries after you take that first step outside, even if you don't, you will eventually form a comfortable habit of taking that first step into a new behavior. **This serves as the best possible foundation for further steps and personal growth in that area.**

In the case of push-ups, the common mini habit is to do one every day. This small step creates a much broader effect than you'd think, because not only will you become comfortable with the idea of doing one push-up, you'll also be more comfortable with push-ups in general and with doing them every day. This is going to make scaling up a breeze. Really. And this is the absolute worst case scenario of the *Mini Habits* system (in that you never do extra).

Chances are that you will do extra sometimes. And the reason relates to basic physics. Newton's first law states that...

1. An object that is at rest will stay at rest unless an external force acts upon it.

2. An object that is in motion will not change its velocity unless an external force acts upon it.

Can you see how this relates? Once you take that first step, you are officially *in motion*. You will find as I have, and as Newton's law suggests (for physics anyway), that once you get started it is almost as hard to stop as it is to keep going. Add to this that nothing is more motivating and inspiring than seeing yourself take action. Put it together and we get a new equation:

One small step + desired behavior = high probability of further steps

The Two Moments Of Resistance

I remember living in Virginia with a cat. When it snowed, we naturally wanted to see how our indoor cat liked the snow. Cats don't like water, but do they like fluffy, frozen water? Nope.

First attempt: We walked out into the yard and tossed her into the snow. Failure. She would stand there motionless and confused for three seconds, and quickly race back inside in disapproval.

Second attempt (later day): We placed her on the outskirts of the snow. Success! She actually walked around in it and explored some.

Your brain is just another cat in the snow, and you can quote me on that because I love out of context quotes. Spring massive changes on it and it will run back to its comfortable routines. But introduce changes gently and in small doses, and it just might be curious (not scared) to explore them more.

Your brain is programmed to resist change, but most of that resistance comes at two particular moments.

Resistance Before Action
Think of yourself as a ball resting on a track, or as Newton's law states, "an object that is at rest." Motivation techniques insist that you get motivated before you move, but isn't it easier just to move forward one centimeter and let momentum help you out? Yes, yes, it's much easier! Move yourself slightly forward to get rolling. Once you're rolling, the equation changes to a more favorable physics formula: "an object that is in motion will not change its velocity unless an external force acts upon it."

We want to be in motion in the direction of our goals as much and as frequently as possible. To do this, we need the first action to be *really* easy, because that is the first wall of resistance in any task. Starting is the hardest part, but that doesn't mean it has to be hard to start. "Hardest" is relative.

When the first action is just a nudge, initial resistance shrinks. Once you take action, there is a second wave of resistance. The strength of this second "wave" depends on how much of an impact your first step had (which varies).

Resistance To Do More
The *Mini Habits* strategy addresses the first instance of internal resistance by requiring small steps to start and by making the total requirement too easy to fail. It keeps you from getting overwhelmed and racing back to your old routines (like a cat in the snow).

But once you start, there's another wave of resistance. In my experience, taking that first step often completely shatters this second level of resistance, especially once you have had some practice. But starting out, it was FAR less frequent. Can you guess why? Think about the brain.

This resistance isn't a mystery. It's a subconscious conflict with my typical behavior. The basal ganglia can be fooled into not resisting the first step, but it still knows what it wants when you attempt to do more. So, when the first step isn't enough to break the resistance, you can take another. The basal ganglia doesn't care to "defend" against small steps, only drastic changes. By changing slowly and taking it one step at a time, you're playing by your own brain's rules.

So when I kept setting mini goals in the one push-up challenge, my brain tolerated it. But once I thought about doing even a 10-minute chunk, my brain said, "No, absolutely not. Play video games, young man. You're grounded." So I said, "But can I just get the exercise mat out?" and it said "Yes." You know the rest.

If you're ever in a situation where you'd like to do more than your minimum requirement, simply continue to use small steps (if necessary). But do not come to expect this every time. Your requirement is small for all of the reasons we're discussing! You don't want to jeopardize your long-term success for a short-term gain. I don't want to scare you into doing too little either, so I'll just say this: if your requirement is small on paper *and in your mind,* you're fine.

Now, let's take a closer look at how mini habits work in the moment.

Mini Habits In The Moment

We just talked about the two *occasions* that we meet resistance (before and during a task or project). Now I want to discuss both common *forms* of resistance—mental and physical.

Motivation can't overcome resistance consistently. It is the sometimes solution. The slogan for motivation should be the quote from the movie Anchorman: *60% of the time, it works every time.*

It isn't just motivation though—using willpower recklessly is equally ineffective. Smart willpower management is key to personal development as smart money management is key to financial success. People working normal, relatively low-paying jobs have become millionaires through smart money management while super athletes making millions of dollars every year have gone bankrupt. If you don't plan your action strategy out, you'll flip-flop between poor willpower and motivation strategies, and end up frustrated.

Here's how mini habits overcome mental and physical barriers. I'll use exercise as the example, since it is such a common desire.

Scenario #1: You have energy to exercise, but don't want to do

it (mental barrier).

Since we're going to skip motivation, we're left with using willpower. But instead of saying you have to do a full workout, we'll just say that you HAVE to do one push-up. It's required. As you have energy in this scenario, this isn't a big deal. And once you start, you're going to find the motivation kick in most of the time.

You don't want to exercise right now in this scenario, but you *do* want to exercise generally in life. These are conflicting desires between present moment feelings and your life values. When you do that first push-up, your life values will often inspire you and overtake your prior hesitation. If not, you may have to set a few more micro-goals like I did in the first One Push-up Challenge, but as you lead yourself along, your mind will adjust to what the body is doing. And each small step you take will make your long-term healthy perspective more appealing.

In the willpower section, we saw how willpower depends greatly on the perception of the difficulty of the task, and when you start "stupid small," the perceived difficulty and willpower cost drop drastically. Once you take the first step, your brain is forced to calculate the *true* difficulty of what a full workout would be like, instead of a biased, lazy brain projecting it to be torturous! If you've ever found yourself thinking *it wasn't so bad* after a workout or trying a new experience, you're already familiar with this phenomenon.

Now what if you go overboard with willpower even after starting small, and burn yourself out? This is the situation that life coaches are terrified of... what if you simply don't have the energy to do it? What if you have a headache? While I'm not promising this as a panacea for all action-stopping ailments, I do believe it is the single best action-based strategy—if anything can work, it's this.

Scenario #2: You don't physically feel like exercising because you're tired (physical barrier).

We think of tiredness as a physical barrier, but it's also a mental barrier. Having no energy usually means you have zero motivation. I've overcome this exact scenario countless times with mini habits. More than 1,000 words of this book were written *while* I had a headache, for example. Not just that, but I was tired and wanted to go to sleep. I was completely unmotivated to write, had very little energy, and I did my 50 words anyway (which grew into 1,000 somehow).

In many ways, it's harder not to do a single push-up than to do one. The challenge is so easy that your pride enters the equation: *I may be stubborn and exhausted right now, but come on, I can do that.* I encourage you to frequently remind yourself of the absurdity of not being able to meet your mini habit requirement(s).

I was productive with a headache because I started small. It seemed literally impossible at first based on how I felt. And in the past, there was no way I would even attempt to write in those circumstances with such a *great* excuse. I would have cut my losses and gave the standard promise to myself to do it later. (As I age, I realize that now is yesterday's later, and that later is a bad plan.) It was the perfect storm though—headache, late at night, and dead tired. I swear my bed was giving me pick-up lines.

"Your REM cycle is beautiful, Stephen," it said. My glazed eyes gazed lustfully at the warm covers, and I replied, "In a minute, honey."

My requirement was so easy that I decided to take a minute to meet it and then quit. Instead, I wrote 1,000 words; I was astonished. It was one of those moments when I realized how powerful this life strategy is.

Can you see how mini habits can make you feel unstoppable? Can you see why I'm confident that mini habits can help nearly anyone add good habits? If I can perform in those circumstances—when I have weak willpower—then this strategy is a good one. The basis of this strategy rests not on my unique experience, but on the science of willpower. My experience coincides with the science. Mini habits are designed for minimum willpower exertion and maximum momentum—the perfect scenario.

Fitting Mini Habits Into Your Life

Are you busy? Do you frequently feel overwhelmed with everything you want and must do? A concern you should have with any system is how it fits into your life. Many habit books (wisely) recommend that you only pursue one habit at a time. This is due to our limited willpower being unable to handle too many habits at once. But who wants to dedicate six months to one area of their life and ignore the other things they want to improve? Habits are so valuable that it would be worth it, but it's frustrating to only focus on writing when you want to get in great shape too. This tension between your current focus and the other areas you want to improve can derail you. This is a huge, largely ignored problem that has been without a solution... until now.

Mini habits are so small and willpower-efficient, that you can have multiple habits at once. Even busy and overwhelmed people can succeed with multiple mini habits. Look at mini habits as your day's foundation—these are things you MUST get done, but they only take a few minutes total to do. After that, you can do anything you want, whether it's "bonus reps" or other activities. It's completely flexible to fit your current lifestyle, but it's the crowbar of personal development, because it can leverage an initially small habit in your life into something much bigger.

Part 5

The Mini Habits Difference

"Victorious warriors win first and then go to war, while defeated warriors go to war first and then seek to win."

Sun Tzu, The Art of War

What makes *Mini Habits* different from every other system out there claiming to change your life? How can this system improve habit development and personal growth over traditional methods? These are fair questions to ask, so here are the answers.

Mini Habits Can Compete With Your Existing Habits

Studies on people attempting to change existing habits have found discouraging results.[24] It turns out that once a habit gets strong enough, even the strongest intentions have a tough time turning it around. In the context of a day, you'll do many more habitual behaviors than it seems, and these habits can interfere with your attempts to add in a new healthy habit.

Where *Mini Habits* trounces other habit programs is in competitiveness. When you attempt to introduce a new behavior, it's like trying to enter a weight-lifting competition without training. There is a ton of competition there already, and even worse, the competition is proven, experienced, and stronger than you. Most habit programs go wrong here. They convince you that you can compete head-to-head with these stronger habits right away. (Sorry, I've got $400 riding on smoking and watching TV.) They tell you to introduce a huge change like going from not writing much at all to 2,000 words per day, or being on the couch to exercising for an hour every day. The problem with this is the cost in willpower. It's a math equation that doesn't work out in your favor, unless you already have a strong self-discipline muscle. If not, you'll suffer "burn out" (and I'll win $400).

The brain resists big changes. Have you ever heard of people saying that you just need to get your foot in the door for employment opportunities? Mini habits are that same concept, but instead of getting into a company, we're talking about your brain. I think of the prefrontal cortex as having a spending allowance before the automatic part takes over. For every task, the subconscious brain looks at what you're asking of it and charges you willpower to get into the control room. You're only allowed to *ask for* so much manual control per day, but once you're in, you're in. Mini habits are low-willpower Trojan horses that can leverage their easy access into the brain's control room into big results. I noticed this when I did that first push-up. It was the same physical action for how I started every workout, but I didn't feel the burden of a workout because I didn't ask my brain for the whole thing.

Small Steps & Willpower Are A Winning Team

The perfect team in personal development is small steps and willpower. As long as you have enough willpower for an action, you can take that action. Small steps require little to no willpower. So it's like having unlimited willpower. You can get yourself to do just about anything if you guide yourself along in super small steps. Try it.

If you resist walking up to a girl to ask her out, decide to move your left foot forward, and then your right foot, in her direction. You'll get there, and she'll ask you why you were "walking so funny." ICEBREAKER.

Live update example: After 3 hours of basketball today, I was exhausted. My brain and body told me there was no way I could write. I was falling asleep. I had no willpower. But I aimed for 50 words, which was too small to resist, and once again I'm well beyond my target now (and awake). Many times when you're tired, engaging your mind or body will wake you up.

Other Methods Will Tell You It's Ok To Let Up Too Soon

The common myth is that you can establish a habit in 21 or 30 days. Some books are wholly based around this false concept. The truth is a bit uglier and harder to predict—18 to 254 days until habit formation, depending on the habit and the person.

Mini habits don't have a specific end date, because we don't know how long it will take to form the habit. Instead, we'll look for signs that the behavior is habit. If your experience is like mine, you could end up developing a bigger habit than you planned. My mini habit of writing 50 words a day has resulted in writing more like 2,000 words per day (though not every day).

Mini Habits Increase Your Self-efficacy

Self-efficacy isn't a term you hear much unless you read behavioral science studies. Self-efficacy is your belief in your ability to influence an outcome. In a two-year randomized trial, baseline self-efficacy was shown to have a significant impact on exercise adoption and maintenance.[25] This applies to people who want to exercise as well as those who *need* to exercise for medical purposes (of course, we all *should* exercise to stay healthy). As researchers note in their review,   "patient compliance with exercise prescriptions is more likely to be successful if exercise self-efficacy is assessed and enhanced."[26]

Self-efficacy helps us achieve goals and create habits, but Psychologist Albert Bandura clarifies that "Expectation alone will not produce desired performance if the component capabilities are lacking."[27]   Believing in yourself isn't enough. Lacking the baseline self-efficacy required for success, however, is extremely common in people who suffer from depression, weak willpower, and repeated failures. If you expect to fail, positive results are hard to come by.

Mini Habits are a self-efficacy-generating machine, and importantly, you can get started successfully with zero self-efficacy. Your daily successes will train you to have high self-efficacy. How can you not believe in your ability to do one push-up per day? You can do it in between these two sentences. And this amounts to strengthening your self-efficacy through practice. Mini habits double as training for believing in yourself.

Remember, your brain latches on to any repetition you throw at it. So a problem many people develop is an expectation of failing to reach their goals. Over time, this crushes their self-efficacy because it's hard to believe that next time will be different (*especially* if you're using the same strategy that failed last time). If you've been feeling hopeless, this is exactly what has happened to you. But...you CAN do it. I'm not being motivational; I'm being logical. You can literally make positive progress in your life. To think otherwise is irrational nonsense, and it comes from training yourself to believe you can't.

Mini habits are the perfect way to start over. No longer will you be intimidated by massive goals. No longer will you be attacked with feelings of guilt and inadequacy for falling short. No, this time you're going to be succeeding on a daily basis. The victories may be small, but one small victory to a defeated mind is a big victory.

Right now, you might be wondering, "How can one push-up a day or writing 50 words a day help me? That's not enough progress to matter."

First, that's wrong—when any small behavior becomes a habit, it matters. A lot. A habit is the strongest behavioral foundation a human can have. It's better to have the habit of one push-up per day than to do 30 push-ups every once in a while. *Only habits can be built stronger and higher.*

Also, you're free and encouraged to exceed your target mark—I blow my targets out of the water on a daily basis now. But it's only because I MUST write a measly 50 words a day that I am inclined to write 2,000. Before this, I didn't write at all on some days. It was my ambition to write a lot that made me write very little. Now I write at least 3x as much as before. It's because I'm no longer intimidated to start. I love my safety net, too. I can call the day a success if I take a few minutes to write 50 words—this is *so empowering*.

Many times, I have planned to "just write my 50" and ended up writing 3,000 words. As I mentioned earlier, I once wrote 1,000 words with a headache and no energy. I felt like Superman after doing that. I looked back on the times I was completely healthy and energetic but wasted time, and then saw what I did with a headache and no energy, and got even more excited to share this book with the world.

Mini Habits Give You Autonomy

In a 2012 job satisfaction survey of 411 people, 65% of American and Canadian respondents said they were unsatisfied or somewhat unsatisfied with their jobs.[28] I think it's partly because of the traditional management philosophy that aims to control employees rather than enable them. Other surveys have found autonomy, or the feeling that you have control and can make decisions, is a primary factor in job satisfaction. A Denmark survey conducted by The European Working Conditions Observatory found that "Almost 90% of male employees and almost 85% of female employees with high job decision latitude are satisfied to a high degree, while only about 56% of those with low job decision latitude report a high degree of job satisfaction."[29] This is a specific example of a universal truth—when a person feels controlled, they shut down. People hate it. Perhaps this is because autonomy is strongly associated with freedom.

This is the downfall of many self-help books. They'll say that you have to sweat blood to get what you want in life. Well, isn't sweating blood a sign that a part of you really doesn't like it? Wouldn't you rather treat yourself well in the process of changing into a better person?

The other extreme of self-help books includes fluffy, motivational BS, and other non-threatening prose to make you feel good. You might feel motivated temporarily, but as we've established, relying on feelings and motivation doesn't work in the long run.

In your journey, you're going to love the weightlessness of mini habits. But this is not a pushover system without structure. It's not a vapid attempt to get you psyched up. You'll set strict daily or weekly requirements for yourself, but they're so easy that your subconscious won't feel controlled by your plans (important!). Then, after you meet your small requirement, you're *free* to do what you want. Without guilt, and without an overbearing burden of heavy goals, you're free to explore these healthy behaviors. It makes the process more fun too, and that is a scientifically relevant benefit!

One study found that when people perceived tasks and decisions to be fun (as opposed to tedious, boring, or difficult), they had stronger persistence.[30] Researchers in this study also noted the powerful impact of autonomy, which you'll notice is a key component of mini habits. After your mini habits, you're *free to do what you want*. Autonomy appears to work by means of activating our intrinsic motivation. Examples they mentioned in which increased autonomy gave better results (each supported by their own study) are morbidly obese people losing weight, smokers quitting, and diabetics controlling their blood glucose levels.[31]

Mini Habits Marry The Abstract & Concrete

The two types of goals are abstract and concrete. An abstract goal is "I want to be rich;" a concrete goal is "I want to make $15 by selling lemonade at 3PM today." Most people strongly recommend that you aim for concrete goals, but it is important to also know your abstract life goals and values (as I have written about before on my blog at stephenguise.com). Abstract thinking helps with abstract goals, but can hinder the self-regulation required for concrete goals.

A study by Labroo and Patrick showed the potential effect moods can have on our thinking.[32] The experiments involved various mood manipulation techniques (i.e. asking people to "think of the best/worst day of their life"), and then tests to measure abstract thought ability or preference. They concluded from the study's five experiments that happiness caused people to think abstractly, which helps us see the big picture, but can create a challenge for pursuing goals requiring concrete thinking.

Another problem is seen from a study by Ayelet Fishbach and Ravi Dhar; it suggests early satisfaction or a high expectation of success can make us feel as if we've already succeeded.[33] Dieters were split into two groups. The researchers reminded only one group of their dieting progress, and then offered both groups a reward choice—an apple or a chocolate bar. Of the group reminded of their progress, 85% chose the chocolate bar compared to 58% of the other group, suggesting an "I deserve a reward" mentality.

A primary benefit of mini habits is being able to do them no matter how you feel, including that sense of pre-goal satisfaction that tends to disrupt progress. Because the requirement is so small, there is no valid excuse—not from happiness or lethargy—to skip it.

Happiness decreases your ability to perform concrete goals, but since the concrete part of mini habits is, for example, just one push-up, it's still easy to do while in an abstract state of mind. It's so small that it requires very little mental energy and attention. And since happiness increases performance and focus on abstract goals, after your concrete goal, you can rely on your abstract goal of "being fit" to make you want to exercise more.

As I've had success with mini habits, I've been happier, and it does make concrete mini habits slightly more difficult to achieve (still easy). But once I start on a mini habit, the relevant abstract goals of writing more, reading more, or getting in great shape are easier to pursue.

Because mini habits empower progress on abstract and concrete goals, people who are generally stronger in one or the other can find success. Remember when in the One Push-up Challenge I had to set multiple goals to complete 15 push-ups? I had to rely on concrete, tiny goals to finish the workout. This flexibility is important for consistency because of the psychological changes we experience on a daily basis. It's being prepared for all possible situations and setbacks. There's almost no situation that will cause a complete failure to meet your mini habits, but there are many scenarios where you'll find yourself exceeding your mini habits. The only time I've failed (just one) of my three mini habits was when I forgot to read and fell asleep for the night. Mini habits are perfectly suited for any mood or situation. You can be happy and motivated, tired and depressed, or even sick, and still complete your mini habits and possibly more.

Mini Habits Destroy Fear, Doubt, Intimidation, & Hesitation

These things are best conquered by action. Taking the first step kills fear over time, if not immediately. I'm no longer intimidated to write. I no longer have guilt about not reading enough. Going to the gym is not daunting now—it's fun. *Fear can't exist if you've experienced something and it wasn't scary.*

Mini habits compel you to take that first step, because it's so easy. And even if you step back into your safe zone right after that, you're stepping out again tomorrow. Eventually, you're going to take a second step too. Mini habits expose you to your doubts and fears in a way that feels safe and empowering. You'll see that exercise isn't so hard and you can do it. You'll see that daily writing is easy and writer's block is a self-fulfilling prophecy. You'll start reading more books. You'll have a cleaner home. Whatever you've been wanting to do will become possible.

Mini Habits Create Insane Bonus Effects Of Increased Mindfulness & Willpower

One of the most important skills a person can develop is mindfulness, which is being aware of what you think and do. Being mindful is the difference between living purposefully and going through the motions.

If your mini habit is to drink one glass of water per day, you'll be more mindful of how much water you drink *in general.* When you have to monitor something every day, however small, it climbs the ladder of your consciousness and you'll think about it even after you've met the requirement. I'm so mindful of my writing now because of my mini habit that I think about opportunities to write all day long. You will simultaneously and naturally develop a mindfulness habit, which will help with all future habit modification (including bad habits).

The next bonus is a willpower increase. Since willpower needs endurance more than raw power, frequent repetition of small tasks is the ideal way to "exercise" the willpower muscle. The stronger your willpower, the greater mastery you'll have over your body.

Many people are slaves to their bodies, responding to every feeling and whim. They believe they can't do things if they don't want to do them at the time. Adding mini habits is a great way to fix this mindset while building willpower.

Enough talk. Let's move to action. The next chapter will show you how to create mini habits to last a lifetime.

Part 6

Mini Habits – Eight Small Steps To Big Change

"If you don't execute your ideas, they die."

Roger von Oech

The real fun begins now. This is the step-by-step application guide to choose and implement your own mini habits. I recommend that you get a pad and pen now to go through these and write down your plans and strategy.

Step 1: Choose Your Mini Habits & Habit Plan

Make a quick list of habits you'd like to have at some point. The important ones will come to mind quickly. This will be your reference list for step one. Visit minihabits.com for ideas.

Note: habit ideas from minihabits.com are already in minified form —you can write down these mini habits now as long as you know the larger habit it represents. One push-up could stand for general fitness or for a larger push-up goal of 100 push-ups daily. Otherwise, write down full-size habits for now.

It's tough to pursue one habit when you have a few *more* habits you're anxious to create. It takes a lot of discipline to ignore everything else for a few months in order to solidly develop one habit. It's worth the sacrifice to build one habit that can last a lifetime, but it remains a challenge.

Good news, everyone. As I've alluded to already, you can build multiple mini habits at once! This is due to their small willpower cost and flexibility. Their "size" will vary, though—both in initial difficulty and how much extra you're likely to do. I have written far more bonus words than I've read bonus pages. Writing is a priority for me, so it's naturally where I put in the most effort. That said, I also read much more than I previously did, and on some days, I read much more than I write. You're going to love this flexibility, because it allows for parties, traveling, and other schedule aberrations.

Lately, I have been pursuing three mini habits with great success. It's four if you count exercise, but that's already a habit—I go to the gym 3x a week. I still track it weekly, but it is no longer a willpower challenge. My brain is more likely to encourage exercise than resist it now.

I would not recommend that you pursue any more than four mini habits at a time (and four might be too much). While these habits are individually easy to accomplish, the larger the quantity, the more your focus will be divided amongst them and the more likely you'll neglect or forget one of them. Not only that, but imagine having to meet 100 tiny requirements every day. Yikes! There is a willpower cost for having to do a certain *number* of things every day. Two or three mini habits will be the sweet spot for many people.

Here are the habit plans to choose from...

One Week Flexible Plan (recommended)
In this plan, you start with one habit and use the *Mini Habits* system for one week. Then you evaluate and choose a long-term plan.

Evaluation at one week: Do you feel burnt out? Do you find yourself easily surpassing your requirement every day? Are you crushing it and craving more good habits? Depending on how challenging it is for you, you can stay with one or add more. Since not all habits are of equal difficulty, defining a set number that works for everyone isn't possible or wise. Also keep in mind that the more mini habits you have, the less likely you are to overachieve in them.

Finally, consider what your most difficult day would be like. Maybe you're driving all day on the road or preparing for a big party—can you complete your mini habits then? Don't imagine the easiest days; imagine the hardest days. If you can do something on the day you're tired, stressed, and very busy, you can do it every day.

Now, if you feel like your willpower can handle an extra mini habit (or two), add it! Notice that I didn't mention your schedule, because your mini habits should take you less than ten minutes *combined* to complete (if you don't decide to do extra). Everyone has ten minutes to spare for something important.

The one-week flexible plan is recommended for people who want to try the *Mini Habits* system, but aren't sure yet what's best for them. This plan will automatically turn into one of the other plans.

Warning: It's important to mark the one-week mark on your calendar to make a firm decision that day about your future plans. Don't allow a gap!

The Single Mini Plan

Do you want to write consistently more than anything? Do you really want to get serious about your fitness? Do you want to dedicate yourself to daily reading? This single mini plan places all of your focus on one habit; it comes with a very high success rate. I started off doing this with the One Push-up Challenge, in which I was required to do at least one push-up every day. If your willpower is as weak as mine was or if you're depressed, one might be all you can handle. You've got to start somewhere!

This is recommended for people who have a single goal that dwarfs the others in importance right now. It's also a good option for those with very weak self control to help them improve it. Remember, you can always add more mini habits, but it's more painful to have to drop one.

Multiple Mini Plan

This is my current strategy and the most advanced one, but that doesn't mean it's too difficult for a beginner to have success with. I have three mini habits, but you'll see that two of them are practically the same thing: I write at least 50 words for anything, write at least 50 words toward a book, and read at least two pages of a book every day. This is in addition to my now regular-sized habit of working out at the gym 3 times a week (which evolved from the One Push-up Challenge). Even with three distinct daily goals, I can complete my entire list easily in less than ten minutes if needed (and never fail).

If you really want to try four or more mini habits at once starting out, be my guest. It could work, but I don't want it to spoil this great system for you if it's too much for you to consistently complete. While each mini habit is super small, it takes some willpower and discipline to do them all every day. And *Mini Habits* aims for 100% success, not 95%. If you fail at just one mini habit, you won't have the feeling of total success, which is important for maintaining high self-efficacy.

Your ideal quantity of mini habits is largely determined by how difficult each one is for you. Drinking water is easier for most people than a fitness habit (even when minified). Habits that involve having to drive somewhere are a *significantly more difficult* option, especially because it depends on availability, location, etc. Mine are easy because I can bring my laptop with me everywhere. Previously, I'd think, *I guess I can't write because I'm going on vacation for 2 days.* Not anymore! Now I can be productive on vacation too (I know what you're thinking, but I can just meet the minimum if I want to relax instead).

The multiple mini plan is recommended for people who have several good habits they're eager to develop or would feel unsatisfied to only develop one at a time.

If you're not sure which plan is best for you, choose the flexible plan and pick one habit for now that you'd most like to form. Don't be afraid to name the full amount of what you want in this step (e.g. exercising 5x a week consistently).

At this point, you should have a habit plan, and full-sized habits to pursue. They may be related to fitness, writing, reading, drinking water, habitual gratefulness, meditating, programming, etc. Now we're going to minify them!

Make Your Habits "Stupid Small"

The reason we tend to resist giving ourselves small steps has to do with societal norms, a habit of thinking bigger, and pride. *I can do 20 push-ups easily*, a person will think, *so there's no need to say I'll do just one.* But this thinking only takes into account one type of strength (physical). Every possible action—such as 20 push-ups—has a willpower requirement attached to it. If you're motivated, full of energy, and in shape, 20 push-ups might not "cost" you much willpower. But when you're a little bit tired already and not feeling up to it, not only will you have less willpower, but the activity will "cost" more of it! A mistake people make when setting goals is not taking into account that their motivation and energy levels are going to fluctuate dramatically. They'll assume that their current state of mind and energy can be preserved or reactivated when the time comes to act. What ensues is a losing struggle against a brain that doesn't want to change (in that way). But this time, we're going to trick our brain and win the willpower game.

My rule of thumb is to minify my desired habit until it sounds stupid. When something sounds "stupid small," your brain sees it as nonthreatening. These are examples that sound stupid small to most people:

One push-up a day? You're joking!

Get rid of one possession every day? Worthless!

Write 50 words a day? You'll never publish anything!

A skill you'll pick up as you practice mini habits is finding creative ways to make your actions smaller and smaller if you feel resistance. If you're resisting your single push-up today—say you have to get in push-up position, or easier, that you have to lie on your stomach on the floor. If your mini habit is to drink one glass of water every day, you can make it smaller by deciding to fill a glass with water, or one step further, pick up a glass. If your mini habit is writing 50 words a day and you're resisting, open up your word processor and write one word. You won't need to do this most of the time as your mini habits are already "stupid small," but remember you have this in your arsenal for times of extreme resistance.

Too small does not exist in regards to mini habits. If you're unsure, go with the smaller option. For ideas of mini habits to implement, visit **minihabits.com**.

This is the key of the *Mini Habits* system. You're going to repeat this *too small to fail* action every day.

Just as important as making your mini habit small is making your thoughts small too. **You must embrace this mini-requirement as if it is a full goal**. This means if you meet the tiny requirement, you're successful for the day. If you can do that, you will get the "big" results you desire.

What To Do With Weekly Mini Habits
I can understand that some things aren't suitable for a daily plan. Exercise is something that many people will want to do 3-5 times a week. Who would want to drive to the gym seven days a week if they're only working out three days a week?

Weekly habits will take longer to form into habit, but they are consistent enough for the brain to recognize as a pattern. So if you *really* want to set a weekly mini habit, try it and see how it works for you. We can do something creative with weekly habits, however, to transform them into a daily requirement. If you want to drive to the gym weekly, as an example, you can set a hybrid mini habit.

A hybrid mini habit is when you give yourself a choice between two options (do A or B). I'm not overly fond of hybrid mini habits because they add to the willpower cost (making decisions also uses willpower), but they are the best option in some cases. And I like that they have you do *something* every day.

Hybrid mini habit examples:

- Drive to the gym OR dance for the duration of one song

- Drive to the gym OR do one push-up

- Drive to the gym OR jog for one minute

With this example, on off days, you have a replacement activity. *Won't people just choose the easy one every day?* First, I think you might be surprised at what you'll do without any additional requirements. Granting yourself freedom in a smart way is very empowering. And you *want* to be fit, right? Second, the mini habit here is just to drive to the gym. If you want to, you can simply drive back home. It sounds crazy, but I must stress the importance of giving yourself a way out of a big, overwhelming 45-minute workout. Your subconscious brain is smart enough to know when a goal on paper isn't your real goal. And it's when we force ourselves into an intimidating commitment that our slow-changing brain rebels.

For a hybrid plans, I recommend starting with no strings attached. Just see how often you decide to go to the gym. If you never seem to choose the gym, then you can start by requiring one gym day per week. Later, you can scale up to two days required per week. Take your time with this though. Don't be in a rush to change, because your brain *can't and won't* change quickly. It will take time anyway, so easing yourself into it is the most logical method.

Alright, now check over your list:

- Do you have a mini habit plan? Did you choose flexible, single, or multiple?

- Are your mini habits "stupid small"? Say them out loud. If you laugh, they pass.

- Is everything written down on paper? Scrap paper is fine.

If so, great! On to step two.

Step 2: Use The Why Drill On Each Mini Habit

Everyone prefers to be healthy, but not everyone is willing to put in the work required to be optimally healthy. There are benefits of eating fast food and watching movies all day too. If your problem has been that you want to do things, but struggle to do them, then you have the right book.

The best way to know if the habits are worth the effort starts by identifying the source. The best habit ideas are sourced straight from your life values. We're not looking for ideas that come from peer pressure and others' expectations for you. If you try to change based on another person or society's opinion, I think you know what will happen, but I'll say it anyway: massive internal resistance.

Using The Why Drill To Get To The Source
Drills drill. That's what they do. And I call the following the "why drill" because the simple question "why?" is the best way to drill down to the core of anything.

Once you've listed your habits, identify why you want them. But don't stop there. Ask why again. Continue to ask why until it becomes circular and repetitive, which means that you've found the core. Honest answers are absolutely necessary for this to work, so dig deep. There will be more than one answer to these questions, so try to pick the most relevant ones. Here are two real and honest examples of mine. One is a great choice to make habit and the other is highly questionable.

I want to write every day. **Why?**

Because writing is my passion. **Why?**

Because it's my favorite way to express myself and tell stories. I can connect with and help people through writing, and I enjoy the process. **Why does that matter?**

Those things make me feel alive and happy. **Why?**

Because writing is clearly something I value and treasure in life. Next example:

I want to get up at 6 AM daily. **Why?**

Because it's what successful people seem to do, and it's embarrassing to get up later. **Why?**

Because I have the sense that society in general and certain people I know look down on me for staying up and waking up later.

In the second example, you can see that the main reason for change is external pressure. That said, getting up at 6 AM could still make me happier. Because of the preconceived notions I have about waking up late and early, it makes me *feel* more successful and decreases my general sense of guilt when I get up earlier. So it's not a throwaway, but when pitted against something like writing (and I'm writing very late at night right now), I'm not going to give it precedence. By staying up late to write, I'm being true to my inner values, even though the world might not agree with it. It's ok if the world doesn't agree with you—don't get bullied into a lifestyle that doesn't suit you.

Step 3: Define Your Habit Cues

The two common habit cues are time-based and activity-based. In a time-based cue, you'll say, "I'm going to exercise MWF at 3

PM." In an activity-based cue, you'll say, "I'm going to exercise MWF 30 minutes after I take my last bite at lunch."

People with 9-5 jobs have very structured schedules, so time-based cues tend to work well for them. Those who have a lot of flexibility in their schedule might benefit more from an activity-based cue that lets them keep a solid, yet flexible schedule. Which cue you'll use depends on your (desired) lifestyle.

Time-based schedules are rigid with little ambiguity (e.g. you start at 4 PM sharp). This helps you to get work done and build discipline. The downside is lack of flexibility—maybe you'll get a headache at 4 PM when you're supposed to do something active. Life has a way of throwing off our schedules. And when you miss a cue and do the task late, you'll hit that awkward stage where you don't know whether to feel successful or guilty.

Activity-based are more flexible with a bit more ambiguity. They help you build structure into a typically structure-less life. The tricky part is in knowing precisely when one activity ends and the other begins. If I am to start writing something after lunch at a restaurant, do I get to settle in and check the mail before I start writing? Must I go straight to the computer? You may think, *that doesn't matter*, but it does, because as the power of mini habits show us, little tasks can easily extend into bigger tasks. Suddenly you'll find yourself organizing your entire desk and remember, *oh yeah, I was supposed to be writing*. Small steps get us started and allow us to build momentum towards a meaningful goal, but it works the other way too. If you allow yourself small concessions, soon enough you'll find them growing against your will.

The question of time-based or activity-based cues isn't all that important. They can both work just fine. What is important is that you choose, and choose firmly. Not making a decision here is a big mistake, but before you lock down your choice, there is one more option that might surprise you. It is my preferred choice for all of my current mini habits.

Freedom-based, Non-specific Habit Cues (General Mini Habits)

Traditional habit books will tell you about the cue-behavior-reward structure of habits from studies, and then proceed to tell you the obvious next step—pick your cue, behavior, and reward. But what if you want to do something like think more positively *in general*? What if you want to do something at varying times? Mini habits open up a new realm of possibility here. The following is especially relevant for flexible schedules and general habits like gratefulness.

Mini habits are rooted in autonomy, freedom, and flexibility. The goal is to *empower* you to have constant success. We can apply this philosophy to restrictive habit cues by instead setting a 24-hour deadline with *no specific cues*.

Have you noticed that bad habits have multiple cues, while everyone suggests that a good habit should have one cue? It's no wonder bad habits are so strong! They have sprawling roots tied to many different cues in your life. That's because bad habits grow naturally through repetition in various circumstances, while we grow good habits artificially with the "single cue-behavior-reward" formula. It's true that if you only have a single cue, you will still be more mindful of that behavior. For example, if you think two happy thoughts at 2 PM every day, then you'll probably think them more in general too. But doing it at 2 PM every day can feel restrictive and forced (depending on your personality). In addition, when you set a specific time to do something, it can feel *wrong* to do it outside of that time. For people who have a morning habit of writing, many of them won't *ever* write at other times of the day. I write at any and all times of day—whatever fits my schedule best.

Another problem with specific cues is their additional load on your willpower. When you have to run at some point today, that's flexible. When you have to run at 3 PM, that's inflexible. The additional pressure to perform the task on time increases willpower cost. Traditional habits suggest you pair this time-sensitive cue with a big task, making it even more difficult for you to succeed. But for us, the total willpower required even for "cue-triggered" actions will still be small because of the mini size of the action. Therefore, mini habits are a better fit into the current popular model of "cue-behavior–reward" than traditionally-sized habits are.

Note: I'm not saying that non-specific cues are always better; they're better *for some people and some habits*. Each habit should be decided on individually.

A general habit is a habit with more than one cue for action. Most of us already have *general habits* of eating, entertaining ourselves, mindlessly browsing the Internet, and so on. Due to the staggering number of cues we experience every day, there's something appealing about not choosing just one cue for a good habit.

The rigidity of having only one cue can hamper social opportunities and spontaneity. But with the dominant habit theories, having one cue is the only viable way to make something a habit. Having multiple cues would require too much willpower, and each cue would need to develop individually, drawing out the process of becoming habit. That's why mini habits are a game-changer.

A general mini habit requires you to do your little requirement once per day, at your leisure. I don't recommend midnight as the deadline, as this is also inflexible. I recommend that going to sleep for the night signifies the end of your day. This gives you the greatest chance to succeed because you can squeeze in your mini habits at the last second. I realize how bad that sounds, but it serves an important purpose in the early stages of mini habits— nurturing your feeling of constant success, which builds your self-efficacy.

I did the One Push-up Challenge for a few months. One of my embarrassingly common cues early on was right before bed (the deadline). This is an indicator of poor discipline because I failed to fit the habit into my schedule during the day. But, instead of going to sleep disappointed, I still went to sleep with a win (and usually, I'd get in some bonus reps too). When you go to sleep feeling like a winner, especially if you do it for many days in a row, it creates an internal desire to improve even more. You've heard that success begets success, right? It's true. Successful people work harder than depressed people because they're already successful. Success ignites passion and action. This is what mini habits will do for you too. You'll feel successful, which will make you want to succeed more and more. I say this not just as the author of this book and the mind behind this system, but as its first guinea pig. I've tried a lot of other systems, and my mini habits results crush anything else I've tried.

Back to the one push-up story: After a while of "stealing wins at the buzzer," I wanted to do better. I began to get my push-ups in earlier. The timing still varied (different cues). This is why it's ok to meet the minimum just before bed. It encourages you to build your own self-discipline. True self-discipline is not when you have someone ordering you to do push-ups, it's *when you decide on your own to do them*. It's SELF-discipline.

Despite my great success in reading, writing, and exercising consistently, it was weird, because I felt like a fraud. I didn't have "habit cues." All of the popular habit books talk about them. The science said they were essential. All I had were daily requirements and a weekly exercise quota. This is supposed to be how people fail their habits, and yet I'm having wild success. Why?

The first thing I realized is that these studies test big, willpower-guzzling goals like going out for a morning run at 6 AM, doing 100 push-ups daily, or sticking with a workout program. Mini habits, I realized, are so different that some of these rules change.

Mini habits are too small to fail, even without a cue.

You'll always have the ability to fit in your habit right before bedtime (mini habits generally take about one minute each to do). And this nightly habit check will become a habit too, which is wonderful because it keeps you mindful of your life. *Did I meet my easy requirements today? Yes. Excellent!* *sleep*

So what happens when you have a habit too small to fail that's without cues? **The development of multiple habit cues.** And this is really exciting. While I love morning routines in particular and may choose to develop one, it's been great to have a *general* habit of writing. Writing for me resembles the structure of a bad habit. I'm sure I have specific cues (one cue I've noticed is after I eat something), but because I have multiple cues, it seems like I just do it randomly.

But wait just a second... if it can take months to form even one habit with a single cue, it must take years to create multiple cues! Nope. Mini habits are minuscule and easy, and remember the study earlier on habit-formation length? It concluded that the difficulty of a behavior is a primary determinant of how long it takes to make it into a habit.[34] This means that mini habits can become habitual much faster than traditional habits can. The caveat, of course, is that when your goal is 50 words and you write 2,000 each day, it might take longer to make 2,000 words a habit. But if you're crushing it to that degree, that's a great "problem" to have, right? And yes, if you don't have one specific cue, your brain will take longer to make it habit. So if you've got ten habits you want to add to your life and are going for speed, it *will* be faster to set single specific cues for your mini habits. On the other hand, if you want to flexibly "weave" something into your identity and schedule like I have with writing, then make it a general Mini Habit.

A recap of cue options:

- General mini habits are done *once per day.*

- Time-cued mini habits are done *at 3 PM, 9:45PM, etc.*

- Activity-cued mini habits are done *after lunch, before work, while driving, after using the restroom, etc.*

A Few More Details On My General Mini Habits Experience

Some people do their writing in the morning. I write at all times of the day. Writing has become a lifestyle habit for me. You know what happens to me now? I'll be watching a TV show and get the urge to *write* (a great, weird thing!). But when I'm watching something with other people, I don't get this urge, because it's a different scenario. I react dynamically and naturally to situations. When a friend was over for a couple of days, I didn't write as much, and that's exactly how I want to live. If that became a recurring issue that was making me unproductive, I could adjust.

As you can see, this has some positive implications for fixing bad habits as well. "Wild" bad habits grow unintentionally, and grow everywhere. You'll have 98 cues to smoke a cigarette, 53 cues to watch YouTube videos, and 194 cues to browse the Internet mindlessly. It's possible to let your good mini habits grow "wildly" like this. Like plants competing for nutrients, your good habits can then crowd out your bad habits. You can see that writing now competes with watching TV shows for me. This is less likely with specific-cue habits, as they're tethered to just one cue. They can be very strong, don't get me wrong, but unless it shares a cue with a bad habit, it will be isolated from it.

A word of caution: You want to be deliberate about what habits you "let grow" wildly. For example, some people can't relax now because they are workaholics. The work habit gets so ingrained into their identity that retirement confuses and bores them. They *want* to work. I've decided that I want to write and write a lot for the rest of my life, so I'm willing to let my writing habit mesh into my identity (same for reading and exercise). But I'm not sure I'd like the same type of habit for bathing (once a day is fine). For that, I prefer a cued habit like showering once I get out of bed. Sleep schedules and meals might also be best structured so as to let the body get into a circadian and dietary rhythm, respectively.

If you want something to become an encompassing part of your life—good examples include thinking positive thoughts, writing, being thankful, exercising/being active, giving to others, minimalist living, etc.—I recommend setting no specific cue for your mini habit. Only give yourself a daily deadline of doing it before you sleep for the night.

If you want a behavior to have a specific, carved out place in your life, set a specific cue for it. Some examples include exercising on specific days, reading before bed, and writing in the morning. Some people like to have their lives very structured, so they might choose only specific cues. It's all up to preference. You can even choose a combination of "wild" and cued habits.

Decision-making In the Moment
Especially if you're choosing general mini habits, understanding the decision-making process will help you to do them when necessary.

People have two states of mind when making a decision. First, we weigh our options, which is called the deliberative mindset. Then we commit to act, which is called the implemental mindset.[35]

The goal is to move to the implemental frame of mind (instead of getting stuck in the deliberative frame of mind).

One advantage of cues is they cut out the deliberative process and help you get more quickly to an implemental state of mind. This is highly appealing. Cues are the key factor in what's known as *implementation intentions*, which are predetermined decisions of exactly when and how you'll do something. Implementation intentions are known to improve goal success. A mini habit with a cue has an even greater chance of success because it does not require much commitment. It's so small that it's a "no brainer."

Mini habits can work without cues too, though; their minuscule size is what elevates them above competing behaviors. So while you'd need to go through the deliberative process without having a cue, you should not get stuck when trying to decide whether or not to do one push-up or write 50 words. It's too easy to think too hard about it. **If you ever find yourself stalling, remind yourself how small your task is.**

Now, write down your selected cues for each mini habit. I like to keep all of mine under the once per day at any time umbrella. This keeps things simple.

Step 4: Create Your Reward Plan

If you're a prisoner hoping for parole, when do you think is the best time for your parole hearing? I'll tell you. It's right after the parole judge takes a food break. A study found that judges ruled more favorably for prisoners just after a food break (presumably, they were more willing to listen).[36] When you view the chart of parole grant rates, there is an obvious spike after each food break. Making a difficult decision like granting parole is a part of ego depletion—the same energy resource that determines our willpower. And food is a proven reward that can restore it.

What do you think would happen if you tried to make a new habit of sticking your face in the dirt and eating some of it? (Let's assume that you *wanted* to build this habit.) You couldn't do it. The obvious reason is *who would want to do that?* But the technical reason as far as the human brain is concerned is *where's my reward?* There is no reward associated with that behavior. It's more like punishment. Your brain would be *very* adamant against this.

If you're not playing sports, exercise can feel like a drag. Most people don't feel like running around in circles or climbing a fake staircase; they don't feel like pushing, pulling, and lifting various heavy objects at the gym. It comes with a feeling of discomfort.

I can say from experience that going to the gym is **three times** more uncomfortable when you're out of shape. It feels like your muscles are saying, *Hey, we were sleeping!* After your hard workout, you get home, look in the mirror, and your reward is...sweat? At this point, your brain is probably asking you where the real reward is.

There *is* a natural reward for the brain when you exercise. In anaerobic exercise, the brain releases feel-good endorphins, also known as "runner's high." Interestingly, weight-lifting causes endorphin release too, but only if it is heavy and intense. Light or medium intensity lifting won't trigger an endorphin release because it doesn't cause the body to switch to an anaerobic state. I like how writer Tom Scheve puts it:

"When your body crosses over from an aerobic state to an anaerobic state, it's suddenly operating without enough oxygen to satisfy the muscles and cells screaming out for it. This is when the 'runner's high' occurs." [37]

Think of the anaerobic state as a retail store during the holiday season. The body isn't keeping up with its normal operations, so it has to go into another mode to meet increased demand.

Endorphins are a nice natural reward for the brain, but they may not be enough of a reward for some people, especially at first. As exercise can feel a bit like punishment, you might need a bigger reward. They use exercise as punishment in the military for a reason!

Exercise has significant primary rewards of sculpted abs, feeling great, and being healthy, but these are delayed from the time you first exercise. Meanwhile, your brain wants cake NOW! Cake is a sensory (or primary) reward because the sugar hits the taste buds and activates the reward center in the brain. Exercise though, offers mostly abstract (secondary) rewards, like walking on the beach with a great body, feeling satisfied with your effort, and other higher-level thinking. Secondary rewards, as you might guess, take longer to "take hold" in the brain.

Reward Association

If exercise's endorphins and the promise of eventual results do not sufficiently reward your brain at first, you need to call in back up. And because the world is awesome, we don't have to play the habits game fairly. What we can do is attach completely unrelated rewards to certain behaviors. After some time, the brain will associate the behavior with the reward, and that's what we want! And later, the brain won't need the (attached) reward.

If you've ever wondered why so many foods include sugar, it might be because sugar is mildly to moderately addicting. Pretty much anything that delivers a reward to the brain can be addicting. It isn't healthy to consume sugar in excess, but consuming small amounts of sugar for the sake of continuing an important habit may be worth the calories. Moderation is the key here.

A creative way I like to reward my brain is with laughter, which releases feel-good chemicals. I'll sometimes follow a writing session by watching the hilarious Bad Lip Reading videos on YouTube. Just for fun, the next time someone sees you watching a funny YouTube video, tell them you're training your brain. *It's science!*

The secret to building habits is to think of it like teaching a kid to ride a bike. At first, you're letting the kid pedal as you ensure them you're holding on. But at some point, you let go and the child rides on without you. Just like this, at first we offer the brain an extra reward after exercise, but eventually the sense of satisfaction and endorphins are enough for it to sustain the behavior on its own. It learns to see the value of these secondary rewards, which are more pleasing and stronger than sugar-laden rewards in many ways, but it takes time.

Sensory (primary) rewards last as long as the experience lasts. But the feeling you get from being in great shape, or doing something positive for 98 consecutive days stays with you. Right now I'm looking at a giant wall calendar full of check marks that reminds me of the progress I've made. It sounds lame to look at checks and feel good, but my brain knows exactly what each of those marks means. In fact, if you want to be happier, one study shows that celebrating wins is the most effective strategy for making us feel good about our lives.[38] That's quite the endorsement for *Mini Habits*, which is based on celebrating and leveraging small wins.

Reward Strategy
It's not all work in exchange for rewards, though. It's fun to live well and there is satisfaction in developing a good habit. That means if you're exercising, look in the mirror after a few weeks and remind yourself how that progress came about. If you're writing, celebrate your beefed up word count. And even if you're only meeting the minimum requirements on these, think of the great habit you're forming to serve as a foundation for more.

But strategy matters too. If you're using the no cue strategy, then you can either seek rewards after you take action or stay conscious of how you feel and reward yourself when you think you need it. Mini habits offer the perk of a greater sense of satisfaction than traditional habits (i.e. a greater secondary reward!). If you think a great accomplishment feels good, know that it feels even better when you did 95% of it as bonus work. Though when you do a lot of bonus work, you might want to reward yourself to encourage *that behavior*.

Abstract rewards such as a sense of satisfaction are largely tied to your mindset. This is why I emphasize that you celebrate your small successes. Success leads to more success, because we like the results and feelings of success. Learn to love delayed gratification too. The anticipation of a bigger reward later is a form of reward that can often conquer the temptation to cash in on a smaller reward now. The more you practice and experience delayed gratification, the more responsive you'll be to it!

My rule of thumb is to keep myself happy while doing this. I know when I'm nearing burnout, and that's when I'll take a rewarding break.

Rewards Appear To Restore Willpower

Rewards encourage repeat behavior, but did you know that they also restore our willpower? Cognitive scientist Art Markman says, "When you stand in front of that buffet table filled with desserts, seek out a friend and have a fun conversation." [39]

It may seem like a puzzling suggestion, but rewards of *all kinds* may be a viable way to restore your willpower.

Based on Baumeister's "ego depletion" concept, multiple studies have concluded that people can overcome ego depletion by restoring glucose.[40] Some scientists, however, wanted to put another willpower restoration theory to the test: rewards. Their theory was that perhaps it is the reward from eating sugar that restores willpower.[41] Sugar is known to activate the reward centers in the brain.

They started with typical exercises to deplete willpower. Then, one group swished a solution sweetened with artificial sweetener and spit it out (artificial sweeteners do not activate the brain's reward centers). The other group swished with a sugary solution and spit it out (which activates reward centers on contact with taste buds). The results showed that the people who swished with artificial sweetener showed no improvement in ego-depletion, but those who swished with sugar did (i.e. their willpower was restored to normal levels).[42] Because glucose levels were not restored, but willpower levels were restored, it appears that at least some part of willpower restoration comes from rewarding the brain. This is good news for people who want to lose weight, as it means that non-food rewards may be effective in restoring willpower.

So when Markman says to "seek out a friend and have a fun conversation," he's telling you to restore your willpower with a brain reward. Then you'll stand a better chance against that chocolate cheesecake (hey, I said *better chance*). Willpower is commonly associated with avoiding bad habits like this, but we also use willpower to force ourselves to do good things, so rewards will help us stick with our good mini habits by encouraging further behavior *and* restoring willpower.

Step 5: Write Everything Down

Writing something down instantly elevates it above all of your other thoughts. One study found that all thoughts (positive or negative) held greater prominence in the mind when written down on paper.[43] The same impact has not been found for typing. You've got to hand write it to amplify it.

Here are some strategies for tracking your progress. In whatever strategy you choose, I recommend that you check off your success before you go to sleep. If you check off your task early in the day, the sense of completion might make you feel less motivated to do "bonus reps." Also, it's a good habit to check it off before bed so that you don't forget.

The Big Calendar (Recommended)
This is the strategy I use for tracking my mini habits. I use a large desk calendar on the wall in my room. I write my mini habits on a nearby dry erase board, and check off every day on the calendar that I complete them (which is EVERY day, except for the gym, which is 3x a week). In the lower left corner of my day boxes, I'll note when I go to the gym. Then, in the upper right hand corner of Saturday's box (last day of the week), I draw a small tick mark.

That way I can look at that corner and instantly see how many times I've been to the gym this week (or previous weeks). It's simple and it works great. Checking off a successful day still feels great after months of mini habits!

If you have a hybrid Mini Habit like driving to the gym or doing one push-up, you can note them by writing G for Gym or P for Push-up. Then you can look back and see how often you've been choosing each.

Another option is a yearly "at a glance" calendar if you're just going to be checking off days. And a smart budget move is to print one of the many free printable calendars you'll find online (tip: simply print out your Gmail calendar). Physically making a check mark makes your success feel more tangible than digital tracking does. Additionally, if you put it in a prominent place where you'll see it often, it's going to make you mindful of your mini habits, your progress, and your success. Don't underestimate the impact of this!

Jerry Seinfeld appears to have been a pioneer in mini habits. He famously marked each day on his calendar with a big X if he completed his joke-writing task. He recognized that daily progress was the key to forming a habit and improving his craft of telling jokes.

He first told young comedian Brad Isaac about his productivity secret before a show one day. Brad wrote about Seinfeld's response in an article for Lifehacker:

> *"After a few days you'll have a chain. Just keep at it and the chain will grow longer every day. You'll like seeing that chain, especially when you get a few weeks under your belt. Your only job next is to not break the chain."*[44]

This is a good summation of mini habits. We don't want to break the chain. And the only excuse for breaking the chain is forgetting, because mini habits are too easy to fail. But forgetting is a poor excuse too, because your calendar will be in plain sight and every night before bed you'll ask, "did I do my mini habits today?" And just to throw this out there, I don't see mini habits as a fad you'll drop in a few months, but as a *lifetime* pursuit. It works too well and is too flexible to quit!

Both writing down your mini habits initially and checking them off as you go is **extremely** important for your success. Don't skip it. Regardless of how you *track* your mini habits completion, I suggest you at least handwrite the habits themselves in a place you can see.

Digital Tracking

Some people will want to use their smartphones, and while I prefer the old-fashioned way, smartphones have some significant advantages. The first is accessibility—people carry their smartphones with them everywhere, even on vacations overseas. The second advantage is in that they allow for visibility and reminders—some apps can remind you to do your mini habits (a concrete cue to take action).

Here are the best apps to use for mini habits on IOS and Android.

Warning: Some apps might suggest that you set a vague goal such as "drink more water." I've seen this exact goal recommended. *Never* set vague goals. How does one "drink more water?" If you swallow a few drops of water in the shower, is that good enough? Vague goals aren't measurable and don't give you concrete "I succeeded" or "I failed" feedback. Concrete feedback is *critical* for reinforcing behaviors. Make your mini habits specific and small. For example, you can set the mini habit of drinking one glass of water (with any of the cue types).

For IOS (free)

If you want to go digital and have an iPhone, I recommend trying the Momentum.cc or Productive apps. They track your daily progress in whatever habits you set and mesh well with the *Mini Habits* system. You'll be able to see how many days in a row you've completed your mini habit(s).

For 99 cents, there is an unofficial Mini Habits app. It's a fan-made app (I wasn't involved in its creation). The app allows you to track mini habit completions *and* bonus reps, which is unique to the *Mini Habits* method.

For Android (free)

I have an Android phone, and if I wasn't using the big calendar, I'd probably be using HabitBull or Loop. They both have an easy-to-understand interface, charts, and statistics, and HabitBull has a widget feature.

Another popular habit-tracking app on Android is called Habit Streak. It allows you to set reminders, which can serve as your daily cues to do your mini habits and/or as cues to check your mini habits before bedtime.

Most apps use a chart to track how many days you've completed. Aim for 100 percent success, with no excuses, but if something crazy happens—and it better be crazy, given the size of these requirements—and you miss a day, it won't hurt you. If you miss two days in a row, something is wrong. These are way too easy to be missing two days in a row. Flukes happen, but they don't happen that often.

Again, don't set vague goals as mini habits. Vague goals are unfocused and meaningless and a terrible idea.

Desktop/Laptop Solutions

I think the best simple habit tracker for the desktop is Joe's Goals (joesgoals.com). It's very simple. You can also use one of the many online calendars.

My friend Harry Che also has a solution for goals/habits called

GoalsOnTrack (goalsontrack.com). Of all the goal systems I've used, his is my favorite. I made a lot of progress when I started using it. There's a habit-tracking feature in his program, so if you're looking for an all-in-one solution to track goals and habits, I'd recommend this. I'm wholly focused on building habits, but not everyone has that desire or luxury.

Overall, I think that mobile apps are a better choice than computer apps, because desktops and laptops lack the 24/7 accessibility of smartphones.

Final Note Regarding Digital Apps

You're going to see ideas for pre-made healthy habits to add from these apps and websites. Resist the urge to start these habits unless they're already minified (unlikely). If you really like one of them, make sure that you minify it before adding it to your repertoire! It looks fun to try doing 100 push-ups per day, but it's less fun when you quit. It's more fun to have one push-up per day as a goal and to blow that tiny goal away for 200+ days in a row. You can find mini habit ideas at http://minihabits.com/mini-habit-ideas/. The page will be updated regularly with new habits and "combo plans." Combo plans are synergistic habits that you can try. They're mainly for fun, so you can call yourself cool names like "The Fit Writer." This combo plan includes these daily mini habits:

- Do one push-up (or another exercise mini habit)

- Write 50 words

- Read two pages of a book

Step 6: Think Small

Why are we making these habits so small when we could aim higher? And what if you stop at your small goal? Is it still useful? Yes, and it has to do with willpower.

The advantage of willpower is that it can be strengthened. Very disciplined people are those who have strengthened their willpower. But that's only to get them started. The extremely fit people you see in the gym don't have to force themselves to exercise anymore. They don't actually need willpower anymore, because exercise has become their brain's *first preference*. When you develop a habit, you'll say, "Brain, we need to exercise," and your brain will reply, "I was already on my way to the treadmill. Try to keep up."

We want to do three things on the road to habit:

• Strengthen our willpower

• Make progress in the present moment

• Not exhaust our willpower

Losing any one of those three things would be a problem: Who is ok with always having weak self-control? Who wants to "train" for 3 months before making any progress in life? Who wants to burn out from willpower exhaustion? Uh...nobody.

Seeing those three tall orders doesn't instill confidence in a possible answer, but small steps satisfy all three requirements. We'll cover them, one by one.

Mini Habits For Willpower Strength

What good is strong willpower if you only have it for two hours a day? We want our willpower to last the whole day. Endurance training at the gym involves lifting lighter weights with higher repetition, which trains the muscle to endure. Mini habits are the same way. We're giving ourselves low-willpower tasks, but with high frequency. It takes very little willpower to do one push-up (perhaps just a sliver more than you'd think though—starting something truly is the hardest part, especially in regards to willpower).

Over time, this frequent repetition of forcing ourselves to perform achievable tasks makes our willpower stronger. It's practice.

Mini Habits For Progress

The biggest question of the *Mini Habits* system is surely regarding the meaningfulness of doing just one push-up a day or thinking one positive thought per day. One way to answer this is to try it yourself and see what happens, but this question still needs to be addressed logically. How can this practice of doing seemingly meaningless quantities of work pay off with real results? There are two ways that it pays off.

A. Mini Habits Bonus Reps: Seeing yourself take action is more inspiring and motivating than anything else. In fact, this is a key strategy of *Mini Habits*—once you're fully motivated to do something, you don't need willpower. Even though we're relying 100% on willpower to do these mini habits, motivation plays a role when we choose to do more than that. I usually find myself highly motivated once I start my habits, but only occasionally *before* I take action. Mini habits aren't anti-motivational; they *generate* motivation. I failed with getting motivated first for ten years, so I'm very familiar with it and slightly grumpy about it.

Whenever I do any mini habit, I almost always do more. And by almost always, I mean well over 90% of the time, and by more, I mean a lot more. Lay's Potato Chips had the famous slogan, "Bet you can't eat just one." Well, I bet you can't do just one push-up or write a few words. Once you start, you're going to want more. At that point, it's as easy to continue as to stop. But what if you don't continue? What if you only meet the minimum requirement every single day? Is all hope lost? No, not at all.

B. The Mini Habits Safety Net (developing actual mini habits): The hope with mini habits is that you'll shoot for 50 words a day and develop the habit of 2,000 words a day, but that may not happen right away. If you stick with your mini habit despite only meeting the small requirement, it will form into a habit, which makes it much easier to do more of it. I know the biggest hurdle for some people is going to be patience. You don't want to be the person writing 50 words a day—you want to catapult yourself into 4,000 words a day and get to your dreams as fast as possible. I have good news for you. If you can write 4,000 words a day, do it. With mini habits, there is no upper limit. Knock yourself out and overwork yourself. *As long as you can meet your mini requirement the next day too, you're fine.*

To conclude, if you can only meet the small requirement, it will still become a habit (and relatively quickly based on the small size). Once it is a habit, you're in perfect position to build upon it. I mean that literally—the *perfect* foundation for doing more of something is having an existing habit of that behavior.

Know this: mini habits *never* hold you back. That would be like saying a spark holds back a fire from starting. Mini habits are sparks with unlimited potential. "Normal goals" might be 2,000 words of writing per day, but that can become a ceiling as well as a minimum. You'll feel satisfied at 2,000 words and say, "That's enough." With my 50-word goal, I have written more than 5,000 words in one day. This is so important to understand, because with the wrong mindset, someone could think that a small goal could hold them back. At some point, that spark is going to become a small flame, and later we'll all be roasting marshmallows over the giant bonfire, telling stories of yore.

If you want progress right now, you'll get it. Work yourself into the ground if you please. And I mention that because many of you are going to be motivated to start off strong.

Mini Habits To Mitigate Willpower Exhaustion

I touched on this in the previous parts, but what makes mini habits great is that you'll never have an excuse for failure, you'll never fear failure, and you'll never feel guilty. Even if you run out of willpower, the requirement is so small that you can find a way to get it done. I can't think of a time when my willpower was so weak that I would be unable to do a push-up, read a couple pages in a book, or write 50 words. Not a single time.

For all of these reasons, small steps don't hold you back—they're critical for success.

Step 7: Meet Your Schedule & Drop High Expectations

Expectations are a tricky thing in life. It's helpful to have *generally* high expectations for yourself, because it increases your ceiling. In other words, if you don't believe you can be in good shape, you never will be (as shown in the self-efficacy study). It's not that belief increases your ability to do things—it increases your willingness to try. If you never try to get in good shape, it's not going to happen!

High expectations of a specific nature, however, such as running eight miles a day or writing 3,000 words a day, are best avoided. A problem you're going to run into is "sneaky swelling" of your targets. Even if you have your mini habits written down in plain sight, your brain might pick up on how for the last 20 days, you've actually written about 1,500 words a day, not 50 words (a personal example from the early days). Your brain is always going to "register" the behavior, not the intention.

Subconsciously, overachievement can set a new expectation in your brain—one that carries all of the weight and pressure of the typical goals you've set in the past (you know, the ones that don't work). So it's vitally important to remind yourself that your daily goal has NOT changed. It's still only 50 words a day. If you're continuing to exceed it, this can feel disappointing, because you won't want to break your 1,500 words-per-day streak. To soothe this concern, remind yourself of how you got to that point (with the low goal) and that you're welcome to continue to write that much if you want, but you are NOT allowed to feel guilty or like a failure if you write 50 words. 50 words is SUCCESS. PERIOD! Not even all caps can stress this enough, because if you get this wrong, then reading this book is a waste of your time. All of the benefits, power, and advantages of this strategy hinge on your ability to keep your goal small on paper *and* in your mind.

If at any time you feel hesitant to meet your goal, check your mind for hidden requirements. Are you really shooting for your mini goal, or has your target grown? **Refuse bigger targets—you can do more with smaller ones.**

Instead of high expectations for quantity of work, we're going to place our expectations and energy on consistency. Life's most powerful tool is consistency, because that's the only way for behaviors to become habits, and when a non-habit becomes habit, it literally means that you've gone from fighting against your brain to joining forces with it.

Step 8: Watch For Signs Of Habit, But Be Careful Not to Jump the Gun

This step is another reminder of patience. The *Mini Habits* strategy works, but if you drop a behavior before it's truly habit and go on to add your next set of habits, then you're going to risk dropping everything like an unskilled juggler. (I am an unskilled juggler, but if I set a mini habit to practice juggling for one minute daily, I bet I would get good at it.)

Signs that it's habit:

- No resistance: it feels easier to do the behavior than not to do it.

- Identity: you now identify with the behavior and would feel completely confident saying, "I read books" or "I'm a writer."

- Mindless action: you'll engage in the behavior without making an executive decision. You won't think, *Ok, I've decided to go to the gym.* You'll just gather your things and go because it's Tuesday, or because it feels like it's time.

- You don't worry about it: starting out, you might worry about missing a day or quitting early, but when a behavior is habit, you *know* that you'll be doing it unless there's an emergency.

- Normalization: habits are non-emotional. You're not going to be excited that "you're really doing it!" once it is habit. When a behavior makes the transition to normalcy, it's habit.

- It's boring: good habits are not exciting; they're just good for you. You'll be more excited about life *because* of your habits, but don't expect it with the behavior itself.

Warning: How to Handle Overachievement

Overachievement is one reason I love this system. We previously discussed how overachieving your target repeatedly can create an expectation to do it consistently before your willpower can support that much work. This is somewhat good and somewhat bad—it's good because your brain is beginning to make it a habit, but it's bad because it raises the bar too soon, which removes the many benefits of having mini habits. Starting small and removing the pressure of expectations is the recipe we're using for success, and it works well, so we want to keep it as long as possible.

Again, I'm not saying you can't do more. If you really want to run five miles today, but your target is just to run out the front door, then that's great! Go ahead and run the five miles, *but don't change your requirement to five miles.* Always be willing to meet your tiny requirement and go back inside (you won't usually choose to go back inside, even being completely free to do so).

If you're not overachieving right away, don't worry. My writing mini habit caught fire right away, but it wasn't until the 57th day that I saw consistently significant overachievement in my reading mini habit. Some mini habit sparks will take longer to ignite than others. It mostly depends on your interest level in the habit and your perceived difficulty in continuing beyond your initial target.

I've written well over my requirement almost every day, but I continue to take comfort in my freedom. I can stop at 50 words. If I have plans, I can meet the requirement in minutes and enjoy my day.

If you overachieve, that's great. If not? That's still great. Not just ok, but *great*. We celebrate all progress, because it's not easy to change your brain. But then again, it is kind of easy to do it this way, isn't it? Compared to wrestling with some massive goal and running on willpower fumes, this is a relative cakewalk with better results.

Part 7

Eight Mini Habit Rules

"Know the rules well, so you can break them effectively."

Dalai Lama XIV

Some rules are meant to be broken. These aren't, but the Dalai Lama quote still applies. Once you master something, you can manage it without rules. The key is in understanding the principles behind these rules.

Since these rules are helpful and positive anyway, you won't need to think about breaking them. In fact, if you find yourself struggling to make progress with your mini habits, it's probably because you're breaking one of these rules.

1. Never, Ever Cheat

There are a few ways to cheat the *Mini Habits* system. The first, most common way to cheat is to give yourself a mini habit such as one push-up per day, but secretly *require* that you do more than the single push-up. The reason why you need to be really, really careful not to do this is because every extra ounce of requirement you put on yourself is going to require more willpower to meet. And while you can likely handle that extra willpower load, you may be pursuing multiple habits at once, and we want to guarantee success, not toe the line of success and failure. You are always allowed to do extra, so let the extra reps come from you, not your requirement. If you want to do more in any session but feel resistance, set additional small requirements after your Mini Habit.

Unlike other habit programs and self-help strategies, discouragement is very rare with mini habits. If you only have to do a single push-up or sit-up, what can stop you from succeeding? It doesn't matter that your goal is small. You're training your brain for success and building up a smaller version of what you hope to accomplish someday (and depending on your eagerness, someday could be very soon!). If your results are like mine, you'll be hitting your bigger targets sooner than expected. But please, please, don't let that raise your expectations. Expect little and you'll have the hunger to do more. When you realize how powerful starting is, and that yes, you had plenty of motivation to do these things all along (which was dormant until you started), life gets very exciting.

2. Be Happy With All Progress

Being happy with small progress is different from having low standards. There's a quote by Bruce Lee that sums it up: "Be happy, but never satisfied." Bruce Lee did more with his limited lifetime of 32 years than two typical people do with 80 years each, so I listen to him.

In Derek Sivers' TED Talk, he showed a video of a man dancing in a field at an outdoor event.[45] The man looked a bit silly out there by himself, dancing wildly to the music. After a few seconds of dancing, another person joined him. Then there were two. After another several seconds, another person joined them. And then another. And when the group reached about 10 people, a giant crowd of people rushed in to join them. Dozens of people were dancing wildly. It is quite the spectacle!

And how did it start? One man danced.

This concept shows exactly what mini habits can do for you. The crowd of people who joined late are like your dormant dreams—shy and scared to take action. They aren't confident enough to dance in the spotlight. That first man dancing is like your decision to take the first small step. Then you notice, *hey, I'm actually doing this right now*. That's when your dormant dreams and passions rush in to encourage you. You already have all the inspiration you need inside of you, but it may be dormant. Awaken it with mini habits.

Mini habits are a pretty simple brain trick at the core, but also a life philosophy that values starting, letting action precede motivation, and believing that small steps can accumulate into giant leaps forward. When you complete a mini habit, it means your mini man is dancing—cheer him on, because he's starting your personal growth party! Celebrate all progress.

3. Reward Yourself Often, Especially After a Mini Habit

What if rewards themselves were rewarding? That is, what if there was a benefit to receiving a reward other than the reward itself? We typically think of rewards as things we get for doing something good, but rewards can give back too. When you complete a Mini Habit and reward yourself—whether it's with food, a fun night out, or a monologue in the mirror about how amazing you are—your reward is going to pay you back by encouraging you to perform your mini habit again.

Ultimately, this creates a positive feedback loop. You will get "addicted" to living a great life, and if that's not ideal, I don't know what is. A perfect behavior would reward you now *and* later. Since most healthy behaviors (like gnawing on raw broccoli) offer limited reward now and greater long-term rewards, it's helpful to attach some form of encouragement to the activity in the early stages. Later, when you notice how great you look and feel, you can assume it's from the broccoli and smile.

Starting is the hardest part, both in the moment and in the early days of habit-building. Initially, you will see limited results. After a hard workout you will feel sore, but look in the mirror and see no change. After eating broccoli, you will feel about the same. After writing on day one, you will not have a full book. But when you do these things over the long haul, you can end up with a fit and healthy body and several full-length novels.

I don't imagine people will forget to reward themselves, but this "rule" is here just in case.

4. Stay Level-headed

Aim for a calm mindset and trust in the process. In these past months that I've seen so much progress, I have not been overly excited and "pumped up." It has been *boring* at times. The difference between winners and losers is that the losers quit when things get boring and monotonous. It's not about motivation; it's about leveraging and conserving your willpower to form lifelong good habits.

The calm mindset is the best mindset for building habits because it's steady and predictable. You may get excited as you make progress, but don't let that excitement become your basis for taking action. This shift to a reliance on motivation/emotions is what foils many personal development plans!

5. If You Feel Strong Resistance, Back Off & Go Smaller

Common "wisdom" tells us that we've got to push through strong feelings of resistance. Well, that's stupid. We've already established that willpower is limited, and if you're pushing beyond your means now, it means you're going to crash and burn later. If you think that you can just do it later as well, then you're not taking into account that you might not have enough desire or willpower to do it later.

Let's picture it. You're sitting down, and you want to exercise, but you *really* don't feel like it. There's intense resistance. What do you do? In this scenario, you don't want to wrestle your brain if you can coax it into doing things your way. Suggest progressively smaller and smaller tasks until the resistance you feel is minimal.

If your goal is to work out at the gym, scale back to requiring yourself to drive to the gym. Say it's really bad, and the best you can do is open your clothes drawer. After you do that, pick up your workout clothes and put them on. If this sounds stupid to you, that's great! When it sounds stupid, that means your brain is giving the go-ahead. These "stupid small" steps slide under the brain's radar like an expert jewel thief avoids security cameras and trip sensors. And before your brain catches on, you'll be on a treadmill at the gym. No step is too small.

The good news is that even if you burn yourself out, the solution for taking action despite burnout is stupid small steps. Burnout is willpower exhaustion—it happens when people force themselves to do too much for too long. But as you're exhausted on the floor, you can appeal to your brain and say, "Hey, could we just do one push-up right now?" After that, you might get motivated to do more, or you could set a few more of these stupid small steps.

If you think this strategy sounds absolutely, completely ridiculous and stupid, it's because you think you can do more. Your pride is telling you that you're better than having to break tasks down into small steps. But every giant accomplishment is made of very small steps anyway, and to take them one at a time like this is not weak, but precise. Before I did the first push-up of the One Push-up Challenge, I felt "above" doing it. I thought that one push-up was worthless (because it's about like clapping my hands as far as exercise goes). But when it helped me exercise for 30 minutes, it changed my mind. So try this out, and see for yourself how you can be nearly unstoppable with this strategy.

When I feel resistance to any task, I make it smaller. Problem solved.

6. Remind Yourself How Easy This Is

When you look at your mini task and feel resistance, you're probably not thinking about how easy it is.

When I was a month into my mini habits, I felt strong resistance to reading my two pages late one night. I was thinking of how much I had read the day before, and assumed that I needed to replicate that. I had to remind myself that the requirement was still just two pages.

Another interesting and encouraging anecdote in favor of mini habits is related to Allen Carr's book titled *The Easy Way To Quit Smoking*. Carr's book has produced greater-than-expected results for helping people quit smoking. And do you know what the basic technique is? Do you know what the difference between Carr's book and most other quit smoking strategies is?

Rick Paulas discusses the surprising success in his article about the book:

> *What's most shocking about the book's contents is perhaps what's missing. There are no stats about lung cancer, heart attacks, or strokes. No scare tactics like what the social pranksters at TheTruth.com dabble in. No veiled threats to the state of your sex life by focusing on bad breath and stained teeth. "The health scares make it harder [to stop]," writes Carr. And are obviously ineffective.*

> *[Paulas mentions how the book repeats]* **Quitting is easy. Quitting is easy. Quitting is easy.**

> *"It's very repetitive," says Tompkins [a smoker]. "And I was aware of that while reading. Like, is this some hypnosis thing?"* 46

Carr's five-hour seminar based on the book has a 53.3% success rate, and that absolutely blows other methods out of the water (other methods have a roughly 10-20% success rate). It's surprising, because it's just information. It isn't hands on. It's not a patch that delivers nicotine to the bloodstream.

And the secret? The key ingredient? The magic?

He gets smokers to believe, consciously and subconsciously, that quitting smoking is easy. When you believe, as many do, that quitting smoking is so hard—doesn't it make sense that maybe your own mind is making it difficult?

Mini habits make you believe that adding healthy behaviors is easy. Even if you're skeptical now, you'll have no choice but to believe when it starts happening.

Forget failures to get motivated; forget epic willpower battles. The bar is so low here that it's possible to never lose. And when you never lose, you tend to win. Over time, your subconscious mind will change, and it gets easier to change your behavior from there.

And let me ask you—why were these (and other healthy behaviors) ever difficult in the first place? What's challenging about typing words? What's so tough about moving your body? What's the big deal with sitting still for an hour to comprehend text? The reason these became such giant challenges in our lives is because we were indoctrinated into a motivation-based society that says you have to get pumped up to live your dreams or do your laundry. Our brains have been trained incorrectly with societal norms, limiting beliefs, and overwhelming goals.

The typical person's subconscious mind is completely feral, dominating the prefrontal cortex, because people run out of energy trying to change their poorly calibrated brain all at once. Mini habits are the way for you to say, *No, you know what? It's not hard to exercise. It's easy. I'm going to drop and do a single push-up right now, and that's really, really easy. It's so easy, I can do it every single day. And I will.* Then you'll be in push-up position, having started, and realize that it's also easy to do one more push-up... and that it's relatively easy to do several more after that. And by that time, you will be inspired to continue because your existing desire to exercise in life will connect with the realization that you *can actually do this.*

I'm excited for you. You're going to realize that easy and hard are relative. Why else would some people struggle to get out of bed and run around the block while others run 100-mile races? It's a difference of the mind. Using most of the strategies available to you today, you're going to struggle mightily to change your brain. They're all based on motivating you or telling you that you can't give in when it gets tough. But that kind of cheap inspiration isn't going to last.

Mini habits are designed to change your brain and your life from the inside out. **Your mini requirement becomes a recurring spark inside of you that will refuse to die out. THAT is inspiring.** You'll be in week three and realize, *wow, I'm still doing this.* In week six, you'll see results (word count, muscle, weight loss, etc.) and prior beliefs about what you could do will shatter before your eyes. As long as you think small, you're going to be a juggernaut. The momentum you build and the mindset shift that will take place will amaze you, as it has me.

Did you know that you're reading proof of mini habits? How did a chronically undisciplined guy write this book *while* writing 4,000-word articles for his blog? I gave myself a small requirement—just write 50 words a day. In the first week, I averaged about 1,000 words. In the second week, 1,500. In the third week, 2,000 words every day. I wasn't trying harder; it was easier than before.

I hope you can see the changes ahead with using mini habits. It's ok to get excited, but excitement won't sustain you. That will be your daily devotion to do the smallest thing in order to make the biggest difference in your life.

If you're skeptical, this is fine too—just give it a try and you'll see.

7. Never Think A Step Is Too Small

If you think a step is too small, you're approaching this from the wrong angle. Every big project is made of small steps just like every organism is made from microscopic cells. Taking small steps keeps you in control over your brain. Small steps are sometimes the only way to move forward if you have weak willpower. Learn to love them and you'll see incredible results!

8. Put Extra Energy and Ambition Toward Bonus Reps, Not A Bigger Requirement

If you're anxious to make big progress, pour that energy into your bonus reps. Bigger requirements look good on paper, but only action counts. Be the person with embarrassing goals and impressive results instead of one of the many people with impressive goals and embarrassing results.

Final Words

An Optional Modification: Increase Mini Requirement Incrementally (Careful!)

There is a modified version of the *Mini Habits* system where you scale up your requirement gradually. I prefer not to do this, because with a greater requirement, you lose freedom, flexibility, and autonomy. I have never found the need to do this with my mini habits, because the requirement only affects me when I meet the bare minimum (and on those days, I'm happy the minimum is easy).

The best reason for you to increase your requirement would be if you find yourself only meeting the minimum day after day. I would still give it at least a month before you try this. If you go a long time without doing extra beyond your easy commitment, then mini habits might not be as effective for you as for others. Don't forget the safety net though—it will still develop into a habit, and a small habit is relatively easy to scale up.

If you work better with a rigid structure, it's something to consider. But until a behavior is habit, it's risky to increase your requirements. If you do, I recommend doing it *very* gradually.

Once you have a habit, you can experiment with higher requirements (such as my normal-sized gym requirement after 6 months of doing one push-up daily). Since you're building off of a strong base at that point, and have built up your willpower, bigger requirements are much more attainable. But again, I would be in no rush to do this if you're getting good results with your mini requirements.

It may be that you need 60 days of meeting the bare minimum before you can leverage the habit. This is how it was with reading for me (as noted, day 57 is when I saw a big improvement).

I first started with one push-up per day, and for about six months I only did about 1-20 push-ups daily. I also exercised at the gym occasionally, but to start, this was all I had to do. In late June, I changed my goal to driving to the gym three times per week. I'm not sure I could have done this to start with (maybe), but I know that doing the one push-up challenge helped me build up my self-discipline and willingness to exercise to make this leap easy.

Apply This Strategy Elsewhere

Mini Habits is more than just a system to teach you how to develop healthy new habits—it's a guide for self-control. Now you know how your brain works, why motivation fails, and how to manage your willpower to make it last. Use these techniques for any situation in which you want to take action. The better you get at mini habits, the more success you'll have in all areas of your life.

This is the end of the book. I hope you enjoyed reading it. I hope the end of this book is the new beginning of a very exciting *Mini Habits* journey for you. I wish you very small successes, over and over and over again.

Sincerely,

Stephen Guise

Email: sguise@deepexistence.com

Want More?

For more mini habit ideas, visit minihabits.com.

My Other Books: *How to Be an Imperfectionist* and *Mini Habits for Weight Loss* are available at all major digital retailers.

Video Course: Readers of this book get a $35 discount on the Mini Habit Mastery Video Course. It contains 3.5 hours of HD video content and features an entire section on eliminating bad habits using the Mini Habits' philosophy. Visit the course on Udemy and enter the coupon code "minibook"

Course Link: https://www.udemy.com/mini-habit-mastery/

For researched and entertaining information on mini habits, small steps, focusing, minimalism, and personal development, visit my main blog, stephenguise.com.

Also consider signing up for my Tuesday messages. These are email-exclusive messages I send out every Tuesday with helpful, life-improving information. And yes, I do like to talk about mini habits a lot. If you sign up, you'll get my first book, *Stress Management Redefined: 8 Steps To Remove Stress Before It Kills You*. It's a short, very fun read at 8,000 words. Lastly, signing up gets you access to my focus toolbox, which has the finest resources around to help you focus. It's all free!

Weekly Messages: http://stephenguise.com/subscribe/

Final note: if you believe this book shares an important message, please leave a review on Amazon. Reviews (in quantity and in rating) are the main metric people use to judge a book's content. And if you have great results with this strategy down the road, please come back and tell other readers (and me) about your success! Every single review has a *huge* impact on others' willingness to read a book, and if this changes your life, you can change someone else's life by spreading the word. The impact of the mini habits idea is up to you.

[1] Nordgren, L. F., F. van Harreveld, & J. van der Pligt. *The Restraint Bias: How the Illusion of Self-Restraint Promotes Impulsive Behavior*. Psychological Science (December 2009). v 20, no. 12, 1523-1528 http://pss.sagepub.com/content/20/12/1523

[2] University of Scranton, Journal of Clinical Psychology (2012). http://www.statisticbrain.com/new-years-resolution-statistics/

[3] Neal, D. T., Wood, W., & Quinn, J. M. *Habits: A repeat performance*. Current Directions in Psychological Science. (2006). v 15, 198-202 http://web.archive.org/web/20120417115147/http://dornsife.usc.edu/wendywood/research/documents/Neal.Wood.Quinn.2006.pdf

[4] Quinn, J. M., A. T. Pascoe, W. Wood, & D. T. Neal. *Can't control yourself? Monitor those bad habits*. Personality and Social Psychology Bulletin. (2010). v 36, 499-511.

[5] Szalavitz, M. Stress Can Boost Good Habits Too. Time Magazine Online. (May 27, 2013). http://healthland.time.com/2013/05/27/stress-can-lead-to-good-habits-too/

[6] Lally, P., C. H. M. van Jaarsveld, H. W. W. Potts, & J. Wardle. *How are habits formed: Modelling habit formation in the real world*. Eur. J. Soc. Psychol., (2010). v 40, 998–1009. doi: 10.1002/ejsp.674

[7] Lhermitte F., B. Pillon, & M. Serdaru. *Human autonomy and the frontal lobes. Part I: Imitation and utilization behavior: a neuropsychological study of 75 patients*. Ann Neurol (1986). v 19, 326-334. http://pacherie.free.fr/COURS/MSC/Lhermitte-AnNeuro-1986a.pdf

[8] (Ibid., Lhermitte F., B. Pillon, & M. Serdaru. *Human autonomy,* 328)

[9] (Ibid., Lhermitte F., B. Pillon, & M. Serdaru. *Human autonomy,* 328)

[10] (Ibid., Lhermitte F., B. Pillon, & M. Serdaru. *Human autonomy,* 328)

[11] Seger, C. A., B. J. Spiering. *A Critical Review of Habit Learning and the Basal Ganglia.* Frontiers in Systems Neuroscience. (2011). v 5, 66.
http://www.ncbi.nlm.nih.gov/pmc/articles/PMC3163829/#!po=15.2174

[12] Knowlton, B J, J. A Mangels, and L. R. Squire. *A Neostriatal Habit Learning System in Humans.* Science 273, (1996). n 5280, 1399.

[13] Dean, J. *Making Habits, Breaking Habits: Why We Do Things, Why We Don't, and How to Make Any Change Stick* Da Capo Press. Kindle Edition. (2013-01-01). p 9.

[14] Wood, W., J. M. Quinn, & D. A. Kashy. *Habits in everyday life: Thought, emotion, and action.* Journal of Personality and Social Psychology. (Dec 2002). v 83(6), 1281-1297.

[15] (Ibid., Dean, J. *Making Habits, Breaking Habits* p. 10)

[16] Muraven, M. & R. F. Baumeister. *Self-Regulation and Depletion of Limited Resources: Does Self-Control Resemble a Muscle?* Psychological Bulletin. (2000). v 126, No. 2, 247-259
http://psyserv06.psy.sbg.ac.at:5916/fetch/PDF/10978569.pdf

[17] Oaten, M. & K. Cheng. *Longitudinal gains in self-regulation from regular physical exercise.* Br J Health Psychol. (Nov 2006). v 11(Pt 4), 717-33. http://www.ncbi.nlm.nih.gov/pubmed/17032494

[18] Baumeister, R. F., E. Bratslavsky, M. Muraven, & D. M. Tice. *Ego Depletion: Is the Active Self a Limited Resource?* Journal of Personality and Social Psychology. (1998). v 74, No. 5, 1252-1265

[19] Vohs, K. D., R. F. Baumeister, J. M. Twenge, B. J. Schmeichel, & D. M. Tice. *Decision Fatigue Exhausts Self-Regulatory Resources.* http://www.chicagobooth.edu/research/workshops/marketing/archive/WorkshopPapers/vohs.pdf

[20] Hagger, M. S., C. Wood, C. Stiff, & N. L. Chatzisarantis. *Ego depletion and the strength model of self-control: a meta-analysis.* Psychol Bull. (Jul 2010). v 136(4), 495-525. http://www.ncbi.nlm.nih.gov/pubmed/20565167

[21] Job, V., C. S. Dweck, & G. M. Walton. *Ego depletion--is it all in your head? implicit theories about willpower affect self-regulation.* Psychol Sci. (Nov 2010). v 21(11), 1686-93. http://www.ncbi.nlm.nih.gov/pubmed/20876879

[22] Berger, C. C. & H Ehrsson. *Mental imagery changes multisensory perception.* Current Biology. (June 27, 2013). v 23(14), 1367-1372. http://ki.se/ki/jsp/polopoly.jsp?d=130&a=165632&l=en&newsdep=130

[23] Hagger, M. S., C. Wood, C. Stiff, & N. L. Chatzisarantis. *Ego depletion and the strength model of self-control: a meta-analysis.* Psychol Bull. (Jul 2010). v 136(4), p 2. http://www.psychology.nottingham.ac.uk/staff/msh/pdfs/mshagger_ego_depletion.pdf

[24] Webb, T. L. & P. Sheeran. *Does Changing Behavioral Intentions Engender Behavior Change? A Meta-analysis of the Experimental Evidence.* Psychological Bulletin. (2006). v 132, no. 2, 249– 268.

[25] Oman, R. F. & A. C. King. *Predicting the adoption and maintenance of exercise participation using self-efficacy and previous exercise participation rates.* Am J Health Promot. (Jan-Feb 1998). v 12(3), 154-61.
http://www.ncbi.nlm.nih.gov/pubmed/10176088

[26] Fletcher, J. S., J. L. Banasik. *Exercise self-efficacy.* Clin Excell Nurse Pract. (May 2001). v 5(3), 134-43.
(http://www.ncbi.nlm.nih.gov/pubmed/11381353)

[27] Bandura, A. *Self-efficacy: Toward a Unifying Theory of Behavioral Change.* Psychological Review. (1977). v 84, No. 2, p. 194

[28] *Majority of Employees Don't Find Job Satisfying.* Right Management. (May 17, 2012).
http://www.right.com/news-and-events/press-releases/2012-press-releases/item23352.aspx

[29] Cabrita, J. & H. Perista. *Measuring job satisfaction in surveys - Comparative analytical report.* European Working Conditions Observatory. (2006).
(http://www.eurofound.europa.eu/ewco/reports/TN0608TR01/TN0608TR01_8.htm)

[30] Laran, J. & C. Janiszewski. *Work or Fun? How Task Construal and Completion Influence Regulatory Behavior.* The Journal of Consumer Research. (April 2011). v 37, No. 6 , 967-983

[31] (Ibid., Laran and Janiszewski, *Work or Fun? p.* 968)

[32] Labroo, A. A. & V. M. Patrick. *Why Happiness Helps You See the Big Picture.* Journal of Consumer Research. (2008).

[33] Fishbach, A. & R. Dhar. *Goals as Excuses or Guides: The Liberating Effect of Perceived Goal Progress on Choice.* Journal of Consumer Research. (2005). v32, 370-77.
http://www.psychologytoday.com/blog/the-science-willpower/2011
12/the-problem-progress-why-succeeding-your-goals-can-sabotage
-your-w

[34] (5. Lally et al., *How Are Habits Formed*)

[35] (15. Vohs et al., *Decision Fatigue,* p. 7-8)

[36] Danziger, S., J. Levav, & L. Avnaim-Pesso. *Extraneous factors in judicial decisions.* PNAS. (2011). v 108, no. 17, 6889–6892
http://www.pnas.org/content/108/17/6889.full.pdf

[37] Scheve, T. *Is there a link between exercise and happiness?* How Stuff Works. p 3.
http://science.howstuffworks.com/life/exercise-happiness2.htm

[38] Quoidbach, J., E. V. Berry, M. Hansenne, & M. Mikolajczak. *Positive emotion regulation and well-being: Comparing the impact of eight savoring and dampening strategies.* Personality and Individual Differences. (October 2010). v 49(5), 368–373
http://www.sciencedirect.com/science/article/pii/S0191886910001
820

[39] Markman, A. *Is Willpower Energy Or Motivation?* Psychology Today. (2012).
http://www.psychologytoday.com/blog/ulterior-motives/201211/is-
willpower-energy-or-motivation

[40] (23. Haggar et al., *Ego Depletion*)

[41] (32. Ibid., Labroo, A. A. & V. M. Patrick. *Why Happiness Helps You See the Big Picture.*)

[42] (32. Ibid., Labroo, A. A. & V. M. Patrick. *Why Happiness Helps You See the Big Picture.*)

[43] Briñol, P., M. Gascó, R. E. Petty, & J. Horcajo. *Treating Thoughts as Material Objects Can Increase or Decrease Their Impact on Evaluation.* Psychological Science. (January 2013) v 24, no. 1, 41-47 http://pss.sagepub.com/content/24/1/41

[44] Isaac, B. *Jerry Seinfeld's Productivity Secret.* Lifehacker. (2007). http://lifehacker.com/281626/jerry-seinfelds-productivity-secret

[45] Sivers, D. *How to start a movement.* (video) TED Talk. (2010). http://www.ted.com/talks/derek_sivers_how_to_start_a_movement.html

[46] Paulas, R. *Quitting Smoking Is Easy When It's Easy.* Outside Magazine Online. (2012). http://www.outsideonline.com/fitness/wellness/Quitting-Smoking-Is-Easy-When-Its-Easy.html